6-10

This Water Goes North

Summer of 1979

May 8: Leave East Leaf Lake,
Minnesota

May 26: Cross the Canadian Border

June 17: Leave Lake Winnipeg

July 12: Arrive at York Factory

July 17: Head for Home

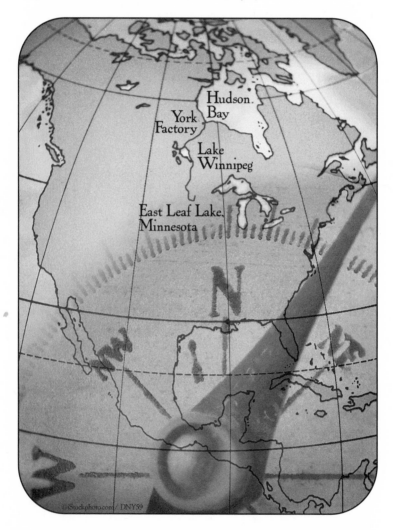

This Water Goes North

DENNIS WEIDEMANN

Adventure comes to those who seek it.

Dennis Weidemann

MÁNITÉNÁHK BOOKS

First Mániténáhk Books edition, 2008.

Interior photos by Hank Kohler and Dennis Weidemann.
Interior design/composition by Linda Weidemann, Wolf Creek Press.

This book is set in 11.75/16 Old Claude, with Emigre's Tribute for display type and Rage Italic for the book's title. It is printed on Glatfelter 60-pound Nature's Book, which is acid-free and contains 30 percent post-consumer waste. ∞

Publisher's Cataloging-in-Publication Data
(*Provided by Quality Books, Inc.*)

Weidemann, Dennis.
   This water goes north / Dennis Weidemann.
      p.   cm.
      SUMMARY: College-age young men embark on a canoeing adventure, traveling 1400 miles from Minnesota to Hudson Bay.
      ISBN-13: 978-0-9796852-0-0
      ISBN-10: 0-9796852-0-6
   1. Canoes and canoeing--Minnesota--Juvenile literature. 2. Canoes and canoeing--Manitoba--Juvenile literature. 3. Weidemann, Dennis--Travel--Juvenile literature. 4. Weidemann, Dennis--Friends and associates--Juvenile literature. 5. Male college students--Juvenile literature. 6. Adventure and adventurers--Juvenile literature. [1. Canoes and canoeing. 2. Weidemann, Dennis. 3. Weidemann, Dennis--Friends and associates. 4. Male college students. 5. Adventure and adventurers.]   I. Title.

GV776.M6W45 2007   797.122'09776
QBI07-600259

Printed in the United States of America by McNaughton & Gunn, Inc.

To Hank, Rich, and Keith...

ॐ

...the world's greatest adventurers,
or at least the finest storytellers.
But then, the two are really the same,
for the storyteller sees living
where others see only life.

R. was referred

ir in 1798, This

the bottom of it.
nipanis River."

goods, etc.

Beluga Whale.
(White Whale)
- Delphinapterus leucas L.
No stranger to the Hayes and
Nelson River mouth area,

Wreck of "Cearense"

to with numerou

Our deepest gratitude to Donna MacKinnon and
Parks Canada for their efforts to preserve the York Factory
Great House and the vast wilderness surrounding the
Hayes River. Much of the world has changed since 1979,
but York Factory still stands in solitude, just as it did
three hundred years ago.

Wreck of

wharf

wrecked Crew of
'elican landed in
vicinity

Marsh Point &
80 foot Beacon

Port Nelson II
established by John Abraham
1683-87 at Walker's point

Old Trail York Factory II
York Factory I

HAYES RIVER

York Factory III
National
Historic
Site

Hay!

In 1684-5, La Martinière
and his men built a fort
2 miles inland of the Ha
on "La Gargousse" rive
a palisade was put u
& enclosed 3 buildings.

Deer hedge where
the french had a
place of worship.

Further upstream,
between Jean-Baptiste
Chouart's place and
La Martinière's fort
Des Groseilliers two
houses.

French Creek (Rivière Gargousse)

Head of
Tidewaters

Fishing Island

The York Factory brand which was
burned or stamped on cases, trading goods

Ten Shilling Creek

Here in 1746, the Dobbs
Galley and the California
wintered; in 1747
the expedition went
upon the discovery of
the N.W. passage

Fort Philipshuck 1682
Two houses built by
Des Groseilliers

Berard's Middle Track &
Hayes River Route map
courtesy of Manitoba
Conservation.

Acknowledgments

❦

Sometimes I think paddling to York Factory was easier than writing a book about it. How does one truly explain the fear of crashing in rapids, or the emptiness of looking upon Lake Winnipeg from a canoe? I've done my best to convey those images, and am indebted to several people for their assistance.

Renée at McNaughton & Gunn and George at Circle patiently answered my many questions about printing and binding. Thanks to Shirley and Mitch at Four Lakes Colorgraphics for bringing faded photos back to life, and to my selection crew—Jim Becia, Pat Hotter, and Robert and Deana Zorko.

A trio of word doctors edited and proofread my unorthodox writing—Heather McElwain, Libby Larson, and Sue Boshers. They made this a better book.

The author's wife normally gets a nod in the credits, usually for resisting the urge to strangle the temperamental author. Linda understands—everything.

Special thanks to Mom and Dad, for letting your kids make their own trails, even when they do stuff like paddle to Hudson Bay.

Mániténáhk

ɋ

MÁNITÉNÁHK, the name given to the publisher of this book, has many origins, contexts, and meanings. It literally means "at the place of strangers." It is derived from the Cree word *ománitéw,* which means stranger. The region around York Factory and the southern portions of the Nelson and Churchill rivers indeed brought together many strangers of the early fur trade. In fact, both the Nelson and Churchill rivers are referred to by the Cree people of the area as *Mánitéwi Sípiy,* which translates "river of strangers." Today, people still come from different parts of the world to take this historic and adventurous trip, and in doing so, live up to the name *mániténáhk*—at the place of strangers.

—Ken Paupanekis

JOSEPH KENNETH PAUPANEKIS is a retired educator who was born and raised in Norway House, Manitoba, Canada. Ken has been a school teacher, school administrator, high school principal, university professor, and school superintendent. He is currently a part-time Cree language instructor for the newly created University College of the North at Norway House, Manitoba.

I thank Ken for sharing his wealth of Cree knowledge with me as I cast about for the perfect name.

Contents

Preface

IT MAY SEEM ODD that four Iowa boys would find
themselves on a fourteen-hundred-mile canoe trip, but
really, it isn't. On any summer afternoon, one out of
three kids is lying on the grass, hitching a ride on a passing cloud to somewhere other than where they are. Our
cloud went to Hudson Bay.

Though rarely a day passes that I'm not reminded of
that summer of 1979, I never gave much thought to writing about it. A book seemed at odds with our simple
motivations, and for a quarter-century we were content
to keep the tale to ourselves. One day I was talking to a
neighbor who always coaxed a few trip stories out of me.
He suddenly stopped and called to his young grandsons,
"You boys should listen to this." On that day I realized
that an adventure isn't just for those who take it. Adventure fuels imagination, and vice-versa—if one withers, so
does the other.

I was still hesitant to write. After all, we weren't famous. Then I thought of my grandpa. Grandpa never saw any action during the war, but I couldn't wait for those days when he would pull up a lawn chair next to mine and recount his Navy roguery. He would tell me of the time when Grandma traveled halfway across the country to sneak a birthday cake onto the base. Or, when every ship's gun blazed at a drone airplane during gunnery training. Grandpa would throw his head back and hoot, "Sheesh, that plane kept right on a goin'." In his modest life lies the beauty of adventure—you don't have to discover new territory or be famous to find it. It is the last pure democracy, and that is its allure. If four yokels from down the street can go canoeing and come home with a story to remember, then anyone can.

For those who ever thought about taking a trip, but never did, I hope that in these pages you find a glimpse of what you were looking for. For those who have yet to depart, here is but one adventure that awaits.

This Water Goes North

CHAPTER 1

"It *Can* Be Done"

NEAR PELICAN RAPIDS, Minnesota, 1964.

Fishing conversations between a father and his boy consist mostly of silence, interspersed with cries of "I got one!" and moments where each sees himself in the face of the other. Boys are eager to grow up, and dads yearn for those days when their biggest decision was whether to use a spinner or the Red Eye. Fishing is one of the few times when daydreaming is guilt-free, which is why many of the world's best ideas begin in the middle of a craggy lake, or under the arching willows of a wandering stream.

It was during one of those lazy days of fishing on Beers Lake that Herb Kohler asked his eldest boy a question: "Do you know where this water goes?"

Eager to demonstrate his knowledge, Hank replied as any native Iowan would, "To the Mississippi River, and south to the Gulf of Mexico." To a Midwesterner, *Mississippi* and *water* are interchangeable.

"Nope. This water goes north, to Hudson Bay."

Hank had studied maps. "Isn't that on the other side of Canada, way up where polar bears live?"

"Yup."

"Wow."

An adult sees a successful geography lesson. A boy sees a canoe trip.

Back at a cabin the family rented for a few days each summer, Hank's younger brother Keith gazed at a small, fading plaque that had hung unobtrusively on a wall for as long as he could remember. It told of voyageurs who paddled pelt-laden canoes across unending wilderness to the remote York Factory outpost on Hudson Bay.

An adult sees a lonely life of labor and misery. A boy sees adventure.

∞

AMES, IOWA, 1977.

Autumn began much as it did for most students at Iowa State University. Sophomores like me were happy to be bottom-feeders instead of the bottom, and even happier to get out of the dreaded triple-occupancy room. Someone had already dropped an old television from the tenth floor onto the cement courtyard below, "just to see what would happen." Though not an abnormal activity on college campuses filled with those seeking enlightenment, only at a school noted for its engineering program would the first generation of mass-produced calculators be whirring to estimate the speed at contact.

On the edge of town, the Towers dorm was set away from the rest of campus, which was exactly why I liked it. To the west was open ground, not yet filled with perfect rows of houses. In the distance, the dirty white top of a grain elevator dissolved into the sky. Slumping at my desk, it was unusually quiet for late afternoon on the ninth floor. A warm breeze, maybe the last of the year, pushed through an open window. Closing my eyes, I leaned back and let the soothing wind massage my face. A weathered canvas canoe appeared amid swaying cattails. I dipped a paddle and the boat surged effortlessly. . . .

Already working on the second of four majors I would sample before graduating, life was vague, and distractions came easily. I suspect many in my hometown would have found this quite disturbing. I was the studious type, destined for traditional life. But, most of the folks back home were unaware that I spent much of my time secretly dreaming of another world—one of birch trees and loons, of quiet wilderness where the soul is bare. Even a Hamm's Beer cartoon conjured up vivid imagery. What could be better than sky-blue waters, bright sun, and northwoods critters loafing all afternoon with a game of interspecies baseball?

Much of my craving for the outdoors was a product of yearly family vacations to a cabin in Minnesota. For a young boy, a lake cabin is loaded with endless crusades, so why go anywhere else? For two weeks every summer, shoes and chores were traded for bare feet and rowboat races. Hot afternoons were spent in the water, battling for title of "Inner Tube King," or paddling three miles to a deserted sandy point for a picnic lunch. Cool days might find us in the dark forest, measuring the trunk of a single massive pine that loggers had spared. When rain swept in, we read comic books while sprawled on the cabin floor, letting imagination fill that day's travel quota.

My restlessness on that quiet dormitory day wasn't provoked by any dissatisfaction for where I was. I liked Iowa, especially in the fall. Gently rolling hills of tall corn and bushy soybeans turn yellow, then brown. Red sumacs light up the ditches. An indescribable fragrance hovers over newly harvested fields. If scent were a color, an Iowa fall would be amber, warm and reassuring.

Neither did I long to escape small-town life. Rural Iowa might not be a vacation destination of the fashionably fabulous, or of anyone else for that matter, but it didn't leave me wanting. Only in a graduating class of sixty-eight students could a nerdy short kid make the basketball squad. Only in a small town could you find the entire high school brass band riding the Ferris wheel during the city celebration, belting out the latest Chicago single as the wheel spun round and round. Rural Iowa was a place where churches overflowed with neighbors seeing you off to heaven, even those who didn't like you all that much (they come to make sure you are really gone).

Big-city ills were hard to come by. Rush hour was from 5:01 P.M. to 5:02 P.M., and fifteen minutes before a home football game. Gangs were rare, unless you counted the notorious Cat Club, a loose organization of brothers and cousins whose single purpose was to climb everything on the farm without getting caught.

Of course, Iowa wasn't a sin-free zone. Some fine drug labs were nestled away out in the country, taking advantage of a common farm fertilizer that is a key component in some recipes. But, except for the occasional batch that got out of control and burned down a barn, we heard little about them. Because the owners couldn't call the fire department for help, the flare-ups were a handy method for stabilizing the industry, preventing it from getting too large.

A stray brothel also marketed its ageless trade, but wasn't publicized with the same zeal as those in Nevada— a policy that led me, at age sixteen, to unwittingly play guitar in one. Yet even then, when asked if the band wanted to get paid, or *paid*, we took the cash. A naïve country boy, I was still a little ignorant as to what *paid* had to offer.

From this almost idyllic climate I sprouted, and had no regrets. I was a normal teenager, albeit a little lost. Nothing pushed me to flee everyday life, but something certainly pulled.

Hearing footsteps in the hall, I slowly opened my eyes. On a corkboard above my desk hung a map of the Boundary Waters Canoe Area, a souvenir from a father to his son, ten years ago. Although the most paddling Dad eked out of his young boys came in anticipation of an A&W barbecue sandwich afterward, I never forgot the pure freedom of traveling to wherever the day took us. Each year, I plotted new routes through the myriad of lakes. Thus far, I had traversed only two short courses.

The footsteps stopped at my door, and I heard a familiar voice. "Hey, I just got a job at Happy Joe's Pizza Parlor." It was Tom, my pal from down the hall. "They're looking for another dishwasher. Hurry, and you can probably get there before they interview anyone else."

A job was part of the Weidemann family college plan. The first year of school was completely on the folks, allowing a new student time to adjust to the rigors of college. After that, we were expected to get jobs and work as much as possible. It was a fair deal, an Iowa kind of fair—compassionate, but sweaty.

∞

HIRED. I LIKED the new job, especially the people who worked there. Tom, who once got a date with a girl after crashing into her car during a snowstorm, worked in the kitchen. So did Big Rick, a soft-spoken engineer who enjoyed playing lacrosse, a game that to my understanding has big sticks and no rules for their use. Manning the drink counter was a big-hearted kid called Little Bill, whose favorite prank was to lie corpse-like in the chest freezer, while some poor unsuspecting waitress was sent for ice cream.

Overseeing these and other characters was Hank Kohler. Raised on a farm in western Iowa, Hank was tall, a little older than me, and sported a full mustache that fit the "old-time restaurant" theme at Happy Joe's. A wide friendly grin accompanied him wherever he went. Hank's hometown was one of the last stops before officially entering the Great Plains, its residents somewhat noted for their tendency to consume fermented drink at the slightest provocation. Affable and a skilled storyteller, Hank was capable of turning the most common narrative into a soda-spitting hoot. Patrons loved him, often acting like groupies as he made the rounds from table to table.

I soon graduated from washing dishes to making pizzas. This promotion also meant that I was no longer the sorority girls' slave to be manipulated with a smile—a role that I found only mildly degrading. During one lull, I was scrubbing the prep table, hanging on the fringes of kitchen conversation. Shy and self-conscious, I rarely joined the banter. Someone began to recount the exploits of a recent day of canoeing, and in an unusually bold moment, I mentioned my paddling in the Boundary Waters.

Hank was filling a customer's glass with Coke, and nearly spilled it as he rushed to hand it back across the counter. His whole face expanded and his eyes glowed. "You know, me and my brother Keith and some buddies have been thinking about paddling from Minnesota to Hudson Bay." Not waiting to see if I knew enough about

North American geography to question his mental competency, he quickly added, "Den, I think it can be done."

As I listened to Hank describe the details, I got excited. "You won't believe this. I just read a book about two guys who did something like that in 1930." A dormmate loaned me the book only weeks before. "Have you ever heard of *Canoeing with the Cree,* by Eric Sevareid?"

"No."

"Hank, it *can* be done."

The rest of that night we talked about Hank's plan and discussed the obstacles that could be expected on such a long trip.

For several months, the topic was an occasional source of conversation, but little more than that. Hank spoke of how they were going to go someday, but it seemed like nothing more than a dream to be savored. Something changed, though, when his brother Keith and Rich Wiebke, a hometown friend of theirs, came to Ames to work for the summer before starting their last year of college.

Keith was cheerful and big—a healthy six foot nine. People were instantly drawn to him, like an oversized umbrella of comfort. Less expressive than Hank, he often chose his words carefully, punctuating them with an array of subtle voice inflections and facial gestures. The two brothers were similar, but different, as only brothers could be. This was apparent when they told the same story. Once they finished arguing about the sequence of events, each gave his account a distinct signature.

Rich was shorter than Keith, but still tall, about the same height as Hank. Topped with bushy black hair and always upbeat, life seldom imposed its will on him. He spoke softly, but was armed with dry wit, the kind that gets funnier with time. You might be sitting alone, and all of a sudden chuckle uncontrollably at something Rich said three days ago. Not a big belly laugh, but one that makes you shake your head and chortle.

With the arrival of Keith and Rich, talk of the trip became more frequent, and the tone more serious. As summer closed and Rich and Keith headed back to school, Hank announced that they were going to do it—he, Keith, Rich, and Jim, another friend from back home.

The final catalyst had been Annie, Hank's newlywed wife. Long strawberry-blonde hair and light freckles gave Annie a country beauty that perfectly matched her personality. Fun-loving but grounded, she kept the sometimes-hectic Kohler world running in a semi-straight line. One fateful night, she spoke the words that inhabit the fantasies of all explorers: "If you don't do this trip now, you never will. We have no kids, so . . . go."

Saint Annie.

Hearing the news, envy flooded over me. My sullenness was surprising, because I had never been a part of the plan, and therefore had no expectations. I hadn't even hinted that I wanted to go, yet now I was consumed by the idea. Being on the outside hadn't bothered me earlier, because, honestly, I didn't think the trip would really happen.

People always talk about dreams that don't materialize. That isn't bad, talking keeps dreams alive. But before, the vision was one I could share. Now, membership was limited. Searching for solace, I let myself believe that my own canoe stories and moral support helped push things along. That wasn't much to go on, but it was something to grasp.

Several weeks after the declaration of intent, it seemed like things hadn't moved very far beyond the original idea. Then, Hank broke the news. "Jim can't go. He's getting married."

Was the trip on hold? Was it done for good? "I might be interested," I blurted.

Even as I said it, I began to build a case against going. How could I afford to take time off from school, or my job? What would my parents think? After all, they were still paying for whatever college expenses my job and loans didn't cover. Did I know these guys well enough? With the wrong personalities, it could be a nightmare. Cripes, two of them were brothers. It would be like throwing them in a box for the summer.

Sadly, most dreams lose to this mental battle of practicality. My personal war lasted two more brutal days. I didn't know it at the time, but Hank had approached the others with similar tentativeness. "I don't know him very well, but he seems okay. Plus, he's got a canoe, and might even know how to paddle it."

Evidently, a canoe and no confirmable jail time were enough, because later in the week, Hank took me aside. "You seriously want to go?" he asked.

Now it was up to me to give the final word. The answers came fast. I decided to take off the spring semester from school and work full-time to save money. College wasn't following my blueprint anyway, and maybe floating down a wild river would help me figure out what I wanted to do in life—a blatant rationalization, yes, but rationalization is a wonderful friend.

When I told Mom and Dad, they said, "Have fun, and be careful." It doesn't matter what age you are, parents always tell you to be careful.

My girlfriend said, "Have fun, and be careful." Girlfriends can be a lot like parents.

One more crucial test remained—Marylou. Marylou was the restaurant daytime assistant manager, and the perfect complement to Hank. Whereas Hank was at ease in the forefront, Marylou handled the daily operational details with superb efficiency. Adorable to those who worked hard, but Satan's first cousin to slackers, you never asked Marylou a question unless you wanted to hear sugar-free truth. As we ate our lunches after the noon rush, I told her of my intent.

She continued to eat for a moment, then looked up, smiled wryly, and slowly shook her head. "You're nuts."

I swallowed hard.

She kept staring at me. "You should go."

So the journey began.

CHAPTER 2

Packs, Paddles, and Provisions

PLANNING PROCEEDED in earnest throughout the winter, with every spare minute devoted to some aspect of the voyage. We pondered scores of vital details, from what should go in the first aid kit to what kind of rope to bring to how many socks to take—we concluded that the proper number of socks is seven; two will be dirty, two wet, two on the feet, and one lost.

The fourteen hundred miles we'd need to cover broke down into three distinct sections. Beginning on East Leaf Lake, just northeast of Fergus Falls, Minnesota, the first leg would run the Otter Tail River to the Red River all the way up to the city of Winnipeg, about sixty miles north of the Canadian border. This part of the trip would be more like a weekend outing (plus three weeks), camping wherever landowners would allow, and picking up supplies every two or three days. We'd even have the requisite cooler for carrying fresh food.

Embarking on our great voyage from East Leaf Lake was particularly significant for us. Not only is the lake near the cabin that the Kohlers rented, it also sits within the Mississippi watershed. Taking off in water that flows to the Caribbean, we intended to end up on the opposite side of the continent. This was mostly symbolic, as we would quickly paddle out of the Mississippi drainage, but it meant something to those of us who had spent our entire lives with Old Man River.

Leg two had a single objective, crossing Lake Winnipeg. Larger than Lake Ontario, it is a beast, nearly three hundred miles long and up to sixty miles wide. Entering from the south, we would quickly leave civilization behind, following the eastern shore up the entire length to Norway House, a village just past the northern tip of the lake.

The third and final leg would follow the Hayes River route to Hudson Bay, passing through four hundred miles of picturesque untamed rivers and lakes.

Our final destination was to be the old York Factory trading post at the mouth of the Hayes River, though we knew sparingly little about it. Most of our information came from history books. In 1670, the king of England granted Hudson's Bay Company exclusive trading rights to all rivers draining into Hudson Bay. To enforce this claim against rival French traders, coastal posts were quickly established. Founded in 1684, York Factory sat at the head of a river system that stretched deep into the continent. Despite the harsh climate and seclusion, the port became the main European trade link to the Canadian interior for two centuries. Birch bark freight canoes, and later, the famed wooden York boats, took blankets and other manufactured goods inland, returning with beaver and fox pelts.

It took us a while to comprehend that native peoples were traveling great distances to trade at York Factory during a time when American colonists were still struggling to traverse the Appalachian Mountains. Equally confounding was that any vessel would sail the Atlantic, into seas that could only be navigated during the short summer months, just to take home a cargo of furs. The skins must have been supple gold.

The post prospered into the mid-1800s, boasting fifty buildings, but southern railroads soon cracked the continental interior, and the decline began. It took another hundred years, but the Hudson's Bay Store closed permanently in 1957. Local Cree who relied on the store relocated a hundred and fifty miles away, and the deserted site became property of the Canadian federal government in 1968. There was still a dot on the map for York Factory, but it didn't sound like much, if anything, was left. We didn't really know.

York Factory wasn't the only source of uncertainty. Curiously, the return part of the trip caused considerable apprehension. Going to Hudson Bay would require fortitude and tenacity, but success depended on us. Getting home was entirely in the hands of someone else. A float-plane was to pick us up at the Bay and lift us to Gods Lake, where we planned to catch a supply plane back to Winnipeg. Or, that was the deal we were hoping to make with an air transport company once we got to Winnipeg.

We set our departure for May 8, 1979. The lakes near Fergus Falls should be free of ice, and the sometimes-shallow Otter Tail might be more navigable in the spring. An early start increased our chances of getting caught in one of the notorious Red River floods, but it gave us plenty of time to hit York Factory during the short ice-free season. Cold weather in the beginning was preferable to the truly severe conditions that might arise at the Bay.

As preparations progressed, two things stood out, neither of which was encouraging: we had a pittance of wilderness experience, and an equal amount of suitable equipment.

In a state where wilderness is defined as anywhere you can throw a rock and not hit corn, Iowa isn't a hotbed for woodsman training. My five-day canoe trips in Minnesota were the closest thing our group had to backcountry experience. Even on afternoon practice outings down docile local rivers, our record wasn't stellar. On one trip, we lost the car keys, and on another, we tipped the beer in the river (a tragedy considered by some to be much worse than losing the keys).

One sporting goods clerk, whose brain I had been picking for information, was particularly unimpressed with our credentials. "You ever been in the bush?" he asked with noticeable disdain.

"No." Afraid of appearing inadequate, I rebounded, "But I've been to the Boundary Waters a couple of times."

This was irrelevant information. "Any of the others ever been in the bush?"

"No."

"You taking a gun?"

"No."

"Is anyone older than you?"

"A little."

As the clerk turned away, I saw his eyes roll skyward. Walking out the door, I mumbled under my breath, "What does he know? He's from Des Moines, even farther from Canada than we are."

Our lack of experience was more troubling to others than it was to us. Youthful optimism is often a by-product of ignorance, and in that we were experts. None of us had ever seen a polar bear, so why worry that we would be camping within a few miles of one of the largest denning sites in the world? We figured that what we didn't know, we could learn along the way—hopefully before anyone was permanently damaged. There was one cloud over all this sunny optimism, and that was Lake Winnipeg. To landlubbers, this inland ocean was foreign and hard to imagine. Mention Winnipeg, and our distant eyes betrayed uneasiness. Of course, there were many other things we *should* have been afraid of, but we were too green to know.

∞

TAKING STOCK OF our gear, it was clear that we were in for the economy version of exploration. We had two canoes, an old Grumman sternback, and an Alumacraft Quetico 17. The Grumman turned easily, but was a bit of a tank. The Alumacraft had an extra-deep keel, which paddled well on lakes, but was very slow to turn. Neither boat was ideal for the diverse water conditions we would encounter. Hank's tent was a discount department store special. I don't remember where mine came from, but it wasn't any better. Cloth sleeping bags were old and of summer weight, rated for no less than forty degrees. None of us owned a decent-sized backpack, either. Of the equipment we piled in Hank's garage one Sunday afternoon, only two quality cypress paddles stood out from the standard weekender stock. Not impressed with the inventory, we came to a crossroads. We could either try to procure sponsors to fund the expedition, or throw together the best outfit we could on our own, and, hopefully, live with it. Sponsorship was tempting, but it seemed contrary to our reasons for going. This was for us, not some corporation. The decision was unanimous. Economy it was.

Our budget came to about nine hundred dollars per person, with the majority earmarked for airplanes and food. That left little for gear. We couldn't afford new tents, canoes, or sleeping bags. We did, however, splurge on four

Duluth Pack canvas packs, and two sets of canoe out-riggers that we thought might come in handy on Lake Winnipeg. Freeze-dried food was a premium item that wasn't in the budget, but we decided to pick out a few packets anyway. This little stash of luxury might be welcome later on, when supply points became scarce. A trip to the camping goods store provided a stroke of luck— all of the food was half price! Employees frowned as we bellowed with delight, which probably didn't foster the "intrepid explorer" image we fancied, but I'm sure Christopher Columbus would have done the same if he had gotten the *Santa Maria* for half price.

What we couldn't afford, we did our best to improvise or manufacture. With just four packs to hold everything, space was limited, so we stored the sleeping bags in water-resistant nylon sacks and attached them to the thwarts with shock cords. We designed canvas covers to snap onto hook-and-eye fasteners drilled into the sides of the canoe, just below the gunwale. They would keep everything dry, and act as a containment system if the canoe flipped. Because I got an A in Boys' Home Economics (where pies only had to pass the palate acumen of a teenage boy), making the covers became my project. For the job, I borrowed a heavy-duty sewing machine from a girl at work. The canvas and leather were rough on needles, and one day the drive belt smoked a little, but I think my home ec teacher would have given me at least a B. Our last purchase consisted of four tiny flags, two American and two

Canadian. They would be proudly affixed to the bow of each canoe.

As the spring of 1979 began, I withdrew from school and worked full-time to earn as much money as possible. I became a "shift vulture," watching for unsuspecting employees who might be looking to give up hours. Sometimes I helped the process along.

"Hey, I hear that the Tri-Delt house is having a party on Friday. You know, the place where Kim lives." Kim was, well, let's just say Kim was Kim.

"I have to work," came the sad reply.

"Oh, really?"

Shameless, but effective. I probably owe Kim about three hundred dollars for all of the shifts I picked up.

With the start date approaching, something interesting happened. People began to ask *why* we were going. To us, the answer was simple. "For fun," we instantly replied. Why even ask such a dumb question? Did anyone actually prefer scraping dried cheese off dinner plates or raking hot asphalt in hundred-degree heat to playing in a canoe all summer? If so, why were these people allowed to vote?

Oddly, some of those who inquired were outwardly disappointed at the absence of a more provocative reason. On the contrary, we could think of none better. Journeys with too much purpose are like rigidly planned vacations, fraught with schedules and tension. Eyes that are so narrowly focused can't see all that each place has to give, nor is there a chance to happen upon an unknown gem and spend a day admiring it. Purpose isn't fun. That's work!

Not everyone understood, but embedded in our simple explanation was the soul of every great quest. Climb a mountain only because it *is*, and all you have done is climb a mountain. An admirable task that may be, but we wanted to climb the mountain to see what it looked like from up there, to eat *shakpa* with the Sherpas. That is where the full wealth of adventure awaits, and we sought its treasure.

CHAPTER 3

Shaken
and Stirred

SPRING CAME LATE and May 8 dawned cloudy, cold, and windy. The Lads from the Southland, as we had come to call ourselves, prepared to depart from a small park at East Leaf Lake. A temporary personnel change brought Annie on board. Rich was still back at home, fulfilling a promise to help with spring planting on the family farm. Annie would sub for him until he joined us two days later at Fergus Falls.

Attendance at the send-off was light, only three hearty souls braving the cold morning. Notably absent was the media, though not for lack of trying to scrounge up a little publicity. A few days before, Hank had walked into a local newspaper office to inform the press of our impending journey.

"Howdy," a friendly Hank greeted. A lady behind the desk looked up.

"Some buddies and I are going to be leaving on a fabulous, fantastic adventure. We're going to canoe from here to Hudson Bay."

The lady smiled. "That's nice."

Uncertain whether she knew where Hudson Bay was, Hank clarified. "We'll spend all summer trying to get there."

"That's nice." She was still smiling.

A little hesitantly, Hank continued. "I just thought that since you guys once ran a story about my little brother Keith canoeing on the Otter Tail, you might be interested."

"Thank you."

Hank shrugged and bid her good-bye, leaving behind directions to East Leaf Lake.

Maybe the reporter went to West Leaf Lake. That's the story we went with anyway.

Undaunted by the press's indifference, we pushed away from the firm shore without fanfare. For our first day, we planned to traverse a few small lakes, paddle the length of Otter Tail Lake, and camp somewhere on the Otter Tail River outlet. It didn't take long to cross paths with history, for it was rumored that North West Company traders, arch enemies of Hudson's Bay Company, established a short-lived post on the north side of Leaf Lake as early as 1778. Technically, a site that drained toward the Mississippi was outside Hudson's Bay Company territory, but this was cutting it awfully close. Not that Nor'Westers would have been bothered either way. Primarily of French and Métis (European/indigenous) stock, they were free traders and felt little obligation to honor England's grant to Hudson's Bay Company.

An early open-field portage of one and a quarter miles was tiresome in a gusting wind that grabbed canoes like sails, but our spirits were still fresh, and easily rebounded from the fatiguing walk. The long portage also presented us with our first chance to cheat when a driver of a pickup offered a lift. We proudly declined, and he continued on his way, noticeably confused. I could hear him thinking, "Dumb kids. Why plow a field with a horse when you have a tractor?"

It was already early evening when we entered Otter Tail Lake, named for its long sandbar "tail." Had the sun been visible, it would be heading down—as was the temperature, which hadn't broken forty-five degrees all day. Unprotected on open water, we began to notice the cold. Whitecaps splashed in from the sides, constantly drenching us with chilling spray, the same water that only days before still contained remnants of winter ice. Unable to stay dry, our bodies grew numb in the wind. Cotton gloves, soaked and heavy with water, were worse than no gloves at all. Despite the misery, we were intent on making it to the outlet, and paddled on.

"Is anyone else getting really cold?" somebody finally asked.

A restrained "yes" came from all corners, spoken with just enough disinterest to maintain an appropriate level of toughness.

"Okay, let's find a place to camp. We aren't going to make the outlet. Look for an occupied cabin, and we'll ask if we can camp there."

Half an hour later, we were still vainly searching for signs of life. It was too early in the season. Few vacationers opened their cabins before the piles of shore ice melted and bare trees sprouted buds. Deserted cottages were plentiful, but we didn't want to trespass, at least not so openly. Another half-hour passed, and the sun temporarily poked its head out to say good night. Twilight made it difficult to see, and the cold continued to escalate. We began to debate the vice of trespass and the distance to the outlet. Just as the risk of jail started to sound good (our cell would at least be warm, and maybe the newspaper would send a reporter for that story), a flag materialized in the growing darkness. Maybe someone was home. Paddling closer, Keith squinted, then cheered, "I've been here before!" Of all the cabins at which to land, this cabin belonged to Orville Nemmers, the father of a girl Keith knew from high school.

Orville was home and insisted that his frosty visitors stay inside for the night. We offered no protest and gathered around a fire, clutching steaming mugs of hot chocolate. Life that had retreated deep into frozen bones slowly reemerged, but only after stubborn protest. Conversation was pleasant, but reserved. The morning's bravado had been whipped into humility. We had overestimated our speed, and got caught in a bad spot. Indecisiveness and pride then kept us on the water too long, way past acceptable parameters for smart camping. Had it not been for Orville, we would be floundering in the wintry dark. It wasn't the epic start we had envisioned.

As we bedded down for the night, legs and toes tingled as blood found its way back home. I wondered how explorers who barely survived one day in civilization would make it all the way to the Bay. It was then that I realized the enormity of what we were about to do, and it was scary. On Otter Tail Lake, mistakes left us cold and hungry. In the Canadian bush, they could get us killed. Our education had begun, and Mother Nature gave homework on the first day of class.

Morning brought a new start, and Orville's tasty breakfast of pancakes and bacon rejuvenated us. We thanked him profusely, especially after learning that the overnight temperature plummeted to well below freezing. Cold and clouds persisted, but as we continued on our way, the Otter Tail River channel offered some protection from the wind.

Linking upland lakes to farm country in the west, the Otter Tail passes through a topographic transition zone of endless variety. Long ago, several glaciers moved through the area from different directions, leaving behind a striking mixture of terrain. Forested hills are interspersed with meadows and reed-filled pocket marshes. Cabins and small farms dot the countryside, ultimately giving way to large farms on the prairie. In one spot, the channel skirts the edge of a shallow valley, and in another, it is squeezed between steep walls. On the second day of our journey, the gloomy morning and nude trees that had not yet blossomed muted the river's beauty.

Several small hydro dams keep the Otter Tail in check. One particularly interesting structure had a U-shaped hole in it. Jagged cement elicited great speculation as to the cause. Had the dam failed? Had it been blown up, the target of some water war? Imagination flourishes on a river. We carefully slipped through the eerie wreckage.

Before it was harnessed for electricity, the river powered flour mills. Remnants of one mill still existed at Phelps, which we portaged around. Driven out of business when it became cheaper to transport raw grain to St. Paul for milling, Phelps Mill had recently been preserved as a symbol of county agricultural history. Fresh out of an Americana painting, a pastoral little park surrounded the building. It beckoned us to stay, but the day was far too young. We kept moving.

A flat spot just below the Taplin Gorge dam holds the honor of being our first outdoor camp. Determined not to repeat the mistakes of day one, we stopped early enough, but still managed to break Hank's camera and burn his new shoes in the fire. Not a good day for Hank. Sleep was scarce, interrupted by frozen everything and the occasional realization that, relative to the water on the other side of the dam, we were about twenty feet below sea level.

As planned, Rich joined us in Fergus Falls, escorted by another Kohler brother. Fergus Falls provided one of the strangest portages of the whole trip. Right in the heart of downtown, the channel slices through a deep gulch blocked with utility pipes and other obstacles.

With no place to carry our gear alongside the river, our chosen route went up to a parking lot, through a busy stop light, across a bridge, and down the drive-up lane of a bank. Motorists gawked, and a surprised bank teller stood openmouthed in the window. Canoe-carrying walk-ups must not be common. We waved to the teller on the second trip, and she weakly waved back, not quite sure about the rough-looking characters outside, but seemingly convinced that a canoe wouldn't be the fastest getaway vehicle.

Winterlike weather continued. Lacking heavy clothing, we futilely layered on T-shirts and sweatshirts, and even donned the coonskin hats that friends gave to us as a send-off joke. Goofy looking they were, but pride is for warm people. Feet and hands suffered the most. Lightweight shoes did little to protect inactive feet resting against the cold aluminum canoe. My hands were so cold that I couldn't grasp the zipper tab on my pants. That may sound humorous, but trust me, it is not. Like a leg that falls asleep, my fingers would not respond, no matter how hard I willed them to. Finally, I stuck my hands in my pants to thaw, much to the dismay of warmer body parts.

With a couple of dams under our belts, they were getting to be old hat. That is, except for the power works project downriver of Fergus Falls. Hank and Keith were still loading up after the portage when Rich and I hollered, "Let 'em buck!" and pushed into the fast water below the dam. Speeding through the tight, curving stream, it was our own personal amusement ride. Flying around one corner, the amusement part abruptly came to a halt. A fallen half-submerged tree stretched three-quarters of the way across the channel. With only seconds to react, we had to choose between attempting an emergency crash into the left bank or shooting for a small gap on the right. We paddled like mad for the gap. Our Alumacraft canoe responded with its usual displeasure for fast turns. Quickly closing on the tree, it was clear we had chosen unwisely.

Slamming into the tree broadside, branches caught our shoulders, and the canoe flipped, toppling us into the water on the upstream side. Taking a quick breath, I hit the frigid water and was immediately pulled down into the underwater labyrinth of limbs. Pinned against the tree and under the canoe, pulling upward to the surface was impossible. The powerful water kept driving me down. If the tree's branches went all the way to the river bottom, there would be no exit, so I held on to whatever I could feel in the darkness. Clawing at the trapped canoe above, I couldn't budge it. I was nearly at the end of my air when I felt the canoe move overhead. It had filled with water, growing heavier, until it created enough force to push some branches out of its way. Like a waterlogged bulldozer, it created a gap and took me with it.

Hitting the surface, my grateful lungs exploded, then gulped in air. Immediately, I scanned the surface for Rich. There he was, floating ahead. "You okay?" I gasped.

"Yeah," came a meek reply.

By the time we corralled the canoe and found solid footing, we could barely stand, our bodies paralyzed from the excruciatingly cold water, minds hazy from shock.

Hank and Keith weren't far behind; as soon as they rounded the bend, they saw our canoe sinking into the tree. In unison, they cried, "They're over!" and plowed headfirst into the nearest bank to avoid a similar fate. Scrambling up the shore, they followed the narrow floodplain that lined the steep bluff, down to where we were struggling to pull everything out of the water. With two soggy companions in near freezing conditions, they quickly set to the business of getting us warm. Wet clothes came off, a tent went up, and a huge fire was started. I was impressed with the cooperation of the two brothers. No disagreements, they did what needed to be done.

In the cold, the searing fire heated us much as the sun heats the planet Mercury, scorching one side while the other is refrigerated. There are two methods for handling this situation: to perform the ancient fire dance, imitating a rotisserie to evenly cook all sides, or to get close enough to melt eyebrows, averaging out the cold in back. I opted for averaging. The shivering eventually stopped, soon replaced with a dull ache in every muscle. Rich was feeling about as good. Finally starting to warm up, I made a feeble attempt to make light of the situation, thinking to myself that the words "wet," "naked," and "forty degrees" should never be used in the same sentence. That was funny for, oh, five seconds.

Once camp was in order, Hank and Keith joined Rich and me next to the bonfire. A scouting party had already scaled the bluff in search of a nearby house, just in case, but nothing was visible through the dense trees. The damage report came in. "The canoe isn't bent, but we won't know if any of the rivets were strained enough to leak until we put it in the water tomorrow. Some things are wet, but we should be able to dry it all out."

I glanced at the sleeping bags suspended on a rope near the fire, and the open tackle box near Hank. A true fisherman, he had ingeniously hung all of the wet lures out to dry on our wire fire grate.

The biggest casualty in the overturn was our confidence. Only after the adrenaline was gone did the reality of danger sink in. Looking at the weary faces glowing in the firelight, it began to hit me. It was the most terrifying thing I had ever experienced. My eyes moved to Rich. Neither of us had said much about how close we came to drowning. Had it been as bad for him? Poor guy, he had only been on the trip an hour and had already almost died.

"Man, this isn't fun," I mumbled, cocking my head toward the faint drone of a car that offered a way out to anyone wanting to walk to the highway and hitch a ride to sanity. The words were more to soothe my shaken pride than they were meant to be taken seriously. Sensing my frustration, Hank and Keith did their best to pick me up.

"It's not your fault, Den," one offered. "You couldn't have avoided the tree from where you rounded the corner. We're all still alive!"

The other chimed in, "And the tarp you made worked great. It kept everything inside."

Maybe that was true, but I felt responsible. After all, I was the one who supposedly had some canoeing experience. I knew that we were unskilled in fast water, and that my canoe would handle poorly. I should have been alert for hazards before they appeared. It could have been a fatal oversight.

In the silence, my eyes darted back to Rich. What would he say?

"Damn it. I lost my hat."

CHAPTER 4

Ramblin' Red

"OH MAN, what's with this?"

The morning after the crash, we stepped out of the tents to find a thin blanket of snow covering everything. For a moment there was dejected silence, then one by one, we starting laughing uncontrollably, especially at Hank's "drying" lures that were now caked with white. What else could go wrong? Scraping off the slushy mess, we packed up wet tents and headed out.

As it winds through the countryside, the river intersects an interstate highway. There's no bridge, just a series of parallel tubes that funnel water to the other side. We figured a portage would be difficult—up a steep incline and across traffic. (I had visions of drivers calculating how many "points" they could get for tagging a pedestrian/canoe combination. It would be a road-hunting bonanza.) Paddling though the narrow tubes looked feasible, but tight. Building on yesterday's lesson, we decided to hike across the road and check the tube exit for obstacles to avoid any surprises. Seeing none, we quickly crossed back to our canoes and ducked into a tube, yelling in the echoing chamber the whole way. As each canoe popped out the other side, a victory cheer ensued. A tiny conquest it was, but a success nonetheless—and we could use a couple more of those.

Even though it didn't feel like spring, birds of all sorts were beginning their yearly rituals. Waterfowl in particular seemed oblivious to the awful weather, which made us envious. An enormous flock of geese patrolled the Orwell Reservoir, so many that landing zones were constricted, forcing the birds into a "drop from the sky like a rock" approach. A goose would glide to where it wanted to land, then crumple like it had been shot. Flailing and twisting to reduce speed, the goose would suddenly pull back into a smooth landing just before hitting the water. It was all so graceful, like a ballet dancer who momentarily slips into a modern jazz routine, then finishes the program with a *fouetté en tournant*. (I admit that I have no clue what that is, but it sounds cool.)

Keith had a personal interest in Orwell, or rather, to get past Orwell. During a teenage attempt to paddle a portion of the Otter Tail, he literally ran out of water here. Late summer drought had left the river too dry. For our adventure, the dam gatekeeper just smirked and said we'd have "*plenty* of water" all the way to Winnipeg. Something about his tone was a little unsettling.

For this leg of the trip, we relied heavily on the good nature of farmers to allow four shaggy drifters to invade their property for a night. Because I was the least imposing of the four vagabonds, the role of ambassador fell to me. I was offended that my image didn't instill the same fear as the great Viking explorers, but sending Keith the Colossal, Rich the Rogue, or Hank the Horrible to an unsuspecting farmer's door might not have netted positive results. Despite efforts to appear nonthreatening on my first diplomatic mission, I saw the farmer's eyes focus behind me, toward the three Yeti lurking by the river. He had kids to protect. Hearing of our pursuit, though, his apprehension subsided, and soon the whole family stood in a semicircle inside the doorway, trying to get a look at the traveling show.

When I returned from that first mission, Keith began a regimen that would stick for the rest of the journey. In an accent that sounded like an unholy mix of German and Norwegian, he would ask, "Vhat ver da questions and vhat ver da answers?"

"This is the Bob Friederichs farm," I replied. "They're really nice. We can camp right here and get water at the pump."

No sooner had I spoken than a child started dumping sticks at our feet, explaining, "Dad said for us to bring you some wood for your fire." Watching our private serfs scamper about, we reveled in the luxury. This must be how kings camped. Scrambling back with another load, one of the little servants bravely approached us. "Are you really going to the ocean?" Landlocked children always seemed unimpressed with our story, until they heard "ocean." Crossing hundreds of miles and international boundaries mean little to a child, but an ocean, now that had to be far away.

Our stay at the Friederichs farm marked the last night on the Otter Tail. Sore bodies, not yet acclimated to day-long paddling, soaked up the kneading heat of the dinner fire. Shoulders felt like tightly wound rubber bands. Butts ached, and knees cramped from being bent in the confines of a canoe. Electric "zingers" shot through our backs. As the fire nursed us, a crisp line of blue sky suddenly appeared in the west. Realizing that the sun was about to shine for the first time in four days, we immediately set about entertaining ourselves by betting on the exact time it would appear. Rules had to be made. Did the first glitter of light count, or did the entire sun have to be exposed? How many judges had to agree? Gliding out only seconds from Hank's guess, the sun embroidered the underside of the clouds deep scarlet. Below, the image softly warped on the surface of the moving river. If this was an omen, it looked like a good one.

∞

A CLOUDLESS MORNING hailed the beginning of a beautiful day, although this splendor came at a price. The clear skies overnight had also allowed the temperature to drop to its lowest point yet, evident in the frozen water hose at the pump.

Stopping for provisions in Breckenridge, we neared a motel. In need of a thorough cleaning, we inquired about purchasing showers. A skeptical clerk rebuffed us, "We don't rent rooms by the hour. We aren't that kind of place." Fast talking and pitiful looks eventually convinced her, for two dollars each. The cost was about half the price of renting the room, but it was worth every penny.

In Breckenridge, the Otter Tail joins the Bois de Sioux River. At this juncture, the channel doubles in size, officially becoming the Red River of the North. This Red River is not to be confused with the Red River of John Wayne cowboy fame. That one is down on the border between Texas and Oklahoma and is probably a lot warmer in May. Hollywood aficionados may be more familiar with the western namesake, but the northern version was equally well known in its time. Long before Texas cows were herded across the southern Red to railheads in Oklahoma, bark canoes loaded with furs destined for European headpieces ran the northern Red to Winnipeg, and beyond. Ironically, railroads initiated the great cattle drives of the old west, and the demise of water trade routes in the north.

A short celebration of paddle waving honored our arrival on the Red River, and the rest of the day transpired in glorious sunshine. How different life is when painted by the sun's pastel brush.

That evening, we chose a battered old house to rest for the night. Seeking permission to camp, I found one of the residents lounging in a drooping shed. On a fence-post near the door, a hand-lettered sign advertised sleighs for sale.

Returning to the crew, I relayed the evening's rules. "We can build a fire to cook." I hesitated. "Oh, and they invited us to play horseshoes and smoke some pot."

The horseshoes sounded like fun, but we weren't sure if the offer was all-or-none. An untimely police raid would definitely hinder our progress. Instead, we stayed at our camp and cooked spaghetti—or tried to. With noodles near completion, we discovered that the sauce was AWOL. Most likely the sauce rested in the river back in Breckenridge, where we'd tipped a grocery sack over on the bank. We contemplated the vast junkyard that must lie at the bottom of the Red, and debated how long an intelligent person would cook noodles before checking to see if there was sauce.

Although we were at long last rewarded with a night almost warm enough to sleep, our precious slumber was disturbed throughout the night by cars coming and going next door. Psychedelic horseshoes must take longer to play than the sanctioned version of the game.

For three more days, we pushed toward Fargo, our momentum temporarily interrupted by a logjam that stretched a hundred feet deep. Recent high water had stacked huge trees like cordwood. The portage wasn't lengthy, and the bottomland was level, but it was mined with that most menacing of Red River defenses—mud. A product of thick silt and clay, the substance goes deep, and is everywhere. To anyone except a geologist, *clay* is a general term for any soil that is undesirable. (I've never heard anyone say, "Hey, come dig in this really neat clay.") And Red River gunk isn't like that nice mud that dries quickly and flakes off. This stuff is foul—a bottomless, slimy, clinging goo, with the lovely fragrance of rotting detritus.

Not all diversions were as unpleasant as the logjam. A lunch break like that in nearby Abercrombie, North Dakota, was more typical. Fort Abercrombie, built in 1858 and abandoned in 1877, was the first permanent United States military fort in North Dakota. It watched over the river and served as a supply base for settlers headed to Montana. Upon our arrival, the aging fort museum and a few dozen houses stood peacefully along empty streets. A lone red Mustang rested in front of a bar sided with half-plank logs. To one side of the door, a Schmidt beer sign hung from a white pole, summoning thirsty patrons. Sitting outside the bar on a wooden step, we drank pop and ate candy bars, listening to the calming stillness of a Sunday afternoon.

Some diversions defied classification. Downriver from Abercrombie, a strange old man was fishing at a check dam. "Do you know where you're at?" he asked.

"Yup." The exact location might be uncertain, but the margin of error was satisfactory.

Eying the flags affixed to the bows of the canoes, he spoke again. "Are you going to Canada, or coming from Canada?" This was curious because he had seen which direction we were traveling. Either geography wasn't his best subject, or we had made one really wrong turn.

∞

RESIDENTS ALONG THE Red complained that spring was nearly a month behind, but at last, winter let go. The weather improved quickly, though broken by sudden and sometimes violent rainsqualls. Trees along the water often hid these tempests until the last minute, and because the river wound about, tracking their direction was difficult. We learned to rely on sound and temperature as much as sight. Thunder might reveal an approaching downpour, or the air might suddenly turn cool, indicating that something bad was in the works. The cooler the air, the bigger the works. Unfortunately for us, nature didn't always fire a warning shot. Rain would suddenly fall out of a petite cloud, or the first crack of thunder would be so close that we nearly tipped over in fright.

Coinciding with better weather, a travel schedule emerged: four hours of paddling, a union-approved half-hour lunch while floating down the river, then four to six more hours of work. This timetable gave us a decent day on the water and enough time to cook supper in daylight.

Each of us began to take on certain duties. I was "Pack," responsible for cramming everything into the rucksacks. Too many packers made it impossible to find anything, and it was inefficient to have everyone standing around, waiting to put something in. And, once again, my height landed me a job. Because I'm short, I could easily keep my balance in the canoe while the others handed over cargo. Ergo, I was also the designated canoe loader. We all helped to set up the tents, and Keith built the fire (I suspect a touch of pyromania there). Hank prepared for cooking while Rich chopped wood and kept us in good spirits. Dish duty was shared, although Keith remarked that his brother was often conveniently off on some important mission during dish time, except when a camera was around.

A normal breakfast to feed the four of us consisted of a pound of bacon and a dozen eggs. Lunch was usually "sammiches," the number determined by Rich's "mich" formula—a complex calculation based on weather, paddling difficulty, and an unknown fudge factor that I think had something to do with phases of the moon. Supper was anything cheap and filling, like spaghetti (preferably with sauce), hot dogs, rice, instant potatoes and gravy, or macaroni and cheese. We could buy ice every two or three days, so the cooler was working out great.

Cooking over an open fire is an art that requires considerable practice. First attempts usually result in some form of blackened recipe. On the upside, hungry people will eat just about anything. A proper fire is essential to success, especially when using aluminum pans that transfer heat easily, as we were. Our method was to build the fire to a roar, using small pieces of wood to produce coals in a hurry, then letting it fall down into an even blanket of heat. Flanked with stones or logs to hold the grate, but not so close as to restrict airflow, we fed the fire carefully selected sticks to maintain coals without producing too many flames. It took only a few scorched meals and soot-covered pots to learn that flames were the cooking fire's— and dishwasher's—worst enemy.

Reckoning ourselves to be rising experts in camping equipment, the flaws in our low-budget outfit became obvious. Wind and driving rain wreaked havoc on the large unsupported sides of my A-frame nylon tent. The rain fly would blow and snap against the sides of the tent, creating a leak wherever it touched. Even heavy dew caused the fly to sag enough to create leaks. The tent's only redeeming quality was that it was big enough to hold Keith. The other tent held up in wind, but its fly didn't stretch far enough to protect the sides, which were not waterproof. A rough fix of duct tape and clear plastic reduced leakage, but made the tent look like a flying saucer. We came to the conclusion that being a tent designer did not require sleeping in one.

We had realized early on that our sleeping bags were wholly inadequate, by a full twenty degrees. The lack of ground mats compounded their ineffectiveness. The bottom side of a sleeping bag loses much of its protective capability when the fluffy filling is crushed under a person's weight; without something insulating the bag from the ground, cold earth stealthily robs the body of vigor. We devised makeshift mats, using boat cushions under the hips and lifejackets under the shoulders. This system helped, but left much of the body in contact with the ground, led to pinched nerves, and required constant readjustment during the night. Nobody slept well that first chilly week. The rough nights we were having down "south" should have raised a dozen red flags, because Hudson Bay was way up north and our knowledge of its weather was a blank piece of paper. For all we knew, it could get much worse, even in the summer. If it did, we would be in serious trouble. But, relief from the cold snap pushed such concerns to the back room: it was hard to think about the Bay when it was still so far away.

Our canoes continued to perform as expected. Hank's stern-back, officially christened "Lucky," wasn't the fastest boat in the fleet, and was sometimes lovingly called the "Barge." The Alumacraft was named "Cad," short for Cadillac. Like a 1970s Cadillac, it rode nice on the straights, but cornered like a school bus.

The homemade canoe covers were the one shining exception in our gear list. Our packs remained inside the canoe during the crash, and stayed dry during bad weather. An added bonus: the rear paddler could stick his feet under the cover when it rained. A flap on the cover hung down from the thwart, enclosing the center compartment and feet. Dry feet are happy feet.

∞

AS WE PADDLED the Red, another routine developed, one that wasn't too popular. It usually invoked the following exchange:

"What direction are we headed?"

"Hmmm." Rich would check the compass that sat on the bow in front of him. "Due south."

"#%&. Again?"

Losing only seventy-one yards of elevation in its entire five hundred and fifty miles, the Red River rambles mindlessly through the flats of prehistoric Lake Agassiz, cutting back on itself over and over, much like the switchbacks on a mountain pass road. Because of this, we could paddle downstream (north) for half an hour, only to end up farther south than when we started. For this reason, northward progress was slow, sometimes only eight to twelve linear miles per day. This worked out to be about one mile per hour, or as we dejectedly calculated one afternoon, three worthless strokes to every good one.

With so little drop in altitude, only one and one-half inches per mile in places, it's no surprise that the land surrounding the Red River is flat. There is Iowa flat, which is more of a rolling hill, and there is North Dakota flat, where a gopher can make some money selling his mound for downhill skiing.

Trees hugged the river, and dotted a few fencerows, but agriculture had claimed most of the black soil for a variety of crops, including wheat, soybeans, and sugar beets. Fields were large, as was the machinery that worked them. Tiny towns speckled the river every ten or twenty miles, but many stayed a mile or two back from the water, presumably for better flood control. Only a bridge suggested their presence in the distance. Many of these traditional farm crossroads probably saw more activity in days past, when farms were smaller and farmers more numerous. Some struggling villages consisted of only the essentials: a grain elevator, church, and a bar.

Away from the river, the horizon was distant and wide. On the river, the channel was often cut deep enough that it was difficult to see far beyond the bank. The muddy water didn't seem suitable for much in the way of recreation aside from catfishing, and, except for a rare johnboat and an occasional angler on shore, people stayed away. Down in the trench, we felt isolated and detached.

It didn't take long for the monotony of the twisting Red to sink in. Especially hard on our morale were openings through the barren trees showing a bend in the river going back the other way. How depressing it was to paddle one direction, knowing that it would all be wiped out on the next curve. Singing and storytelling, an indicator of esprit de corps, began to degrade in quantity and quality.

One night, I ended my journal entry with, "The Red River is the most winding, muddiest, and generally stinking river in the world." A bit unfair, because I had only paddled four rivers, but I was convinced it would make the top ten.

To break the boredom, we occasionally walked or hitched a ride to a restaurant or bar for an evening meal. Rides were easy to come by, people being generous and openly curious about what we were doing. Just outside of Fargo, we got a twofer—a camping spot and a lift—from a young couple who lived in a house abutting the river. Bill and Pam tendered their yard for tents, then kindly drove us to a bar in Wild Rice, North Dakota. Housed in a low building at the end of a short gravel road, the bar *was* Wild Rice. It was just our kind of spot, full of local personality.

These departures from the daily toil gave us a chance to see what was going on outside of our trough, although it took me a while to get used to the thought of seeking people out. On every other canoe trip I had been on, the intent was to get away from them (no offense to the rest of humanity). But this was different. We'd have plenty of opportunity for solitude later in the trip, and it was a waste to stay hidden at the river when we could learn so much about its residents.

∞

CITIES, COMPLETE WITH modern services, may appear to be oases for weary canoeists, but they can be the most challenging of campsites. City parks normally close at dusk, and prohibit ground fires. Transportation systems are built for cars, not feet. Noise rendered inaudible by the walls of a house is unabated by a tent. Unattended canoes are easy targets for thieves. Fortunately, the city of Fargo had us covered in two ways—a park offered overnight camping, and my older brother, Alan, a student at North Dakota State University, met us with my car, which he had retrieved from East Leaf Lake the week before. He and his wife Joy lived just across the river in Moorhead. Accustomed to moving at a pace dictated by physiology, we admired the wondrous automotive technology, although it is debatable how much wonder existed in a rusting 1966 Ford Galaxy 500.

Taking advantage of our newfound mobility, we hit Alan and Joy's place for showers, then found a grocery store, Laundromat, and a pizza parlor. It was good to see Alan. Three years older than me, he was working on his master's degree in limnology, the study of freshwater. He got the scientific brain in the family and set standards at our school that will probably endure forever. Naturally, this meant that his two younger brothers had to deal with high expectations, although it worked to our advantage that he nearly burned down the high school with some warped experiment. He later became a researcher for the Navy, where I think they have a category on the application for "things you've burned or blown up."

Being avid fishermen, Rich, Hank, and Keith probed Alan about potential on the Red. We had fears about what kind of mutants survived in the murk, so they sought Alan's expertise.

"Is it safe to eat the fish?"

Alan chuckled, "Heh-heh. I wouldn't. The water's loaded with farm chemicals."

Resolute, the boys kept pressing. "We won't die or anything, will we?"

Tilting his head down and looking over the glasses that sat low on his nose, Alan realized he was dealing with fishermen. To them, risk is relative to how big or tasty the fish are. Recognizing the futility of his previous recommendation, Alan offered a new safety standard.

"If it don't smell like fish, don't eat it."

Profound advice from one of the world's great scientific minds, this seemed to satisfy the anglers.

In the morning, we set off again, paddling through downtown Fargo, and quickly coming upon the check dam that Alan had warned us about. Check dams are deceptively dangerous. An overturned canoe can be flattened around pilings like tinfoil. Occupants thrown over the dam can hit cement below, or drown in swirling currents. From a distance, the dam appeared completely submerged under high water, but we pulled off to take a look anyway. Rich walked closer for a better view, and reported a series of large rolling waves where the dam should have been. He said he couldn't see any part of the dam, except for a cement pillbox on shore. But the question was, how far below the surface was it? The water was too dirty to see more than three inches down, and our canoes rode deeper than that. If we rammed the top edge of the dam, it could be deadly. A portage would be easy, but it had been four days since anyone had almost died, and our confidence was on the rise. With an emphatic salute to the north, Rich gave the go-ahead. We bounced through the turbulence without incident, and basked in another small success.

Further downstream, still giddy with excitement, we barely noticed a slim figure propped against the embankment of a bridge. It was Alan, leisurely drinking a milkshake. In a city bustling in daily normalcy, oblivious to the river moving through it, he stood alone. As we drifted by, my older sibling offered no fancy words of wisdom, just some friendly bantering. Yet, as we passed, I felt strangely proud. His being there to see us on our way said it all.

We approached a bend in the river, and I looked back one last time. He still leaned against the bridge. I turned forward, feeling newly exhilarated. Until we had hit Fargo, we had been heading toward something we knew. Each stroke now left that world behind.

CHAPTER 5

Plenty of Water

"WINNIPEG'S JUST AROUND the corner, boys!"

With a coarse laugh, our host banged on the tents and repeated his exhortation. Still sleepy from an unnerving gale that hit in the night, we rubbed swollen eyes as we fumbled our way out of bed.

"What time is it?" I stammered.

Rich tried to focus on his watch. "I think it's five o'clock."

"Who ordered the wake-up call for this hour?" I watched for signs of guilt, but everyone looked as bedraggled as me. Evidently we would need to be more careful when telling an aging farmer that we would be leaving "in the morning."

The sweeping bends of the Red River continued to grow wider, but didn't get any straighter. Days were tiring, but relaxing evenings offered us time to recover. Just past Perley, Minnesota, we christened a particularly quiet camp the "bed of coals" night. A supply of beer, courtesy of a midday hitchhiking expedition, and a hissing fire of coals that pulsed yellow and orange provided the perfect setting for introspection and prophesying. Anyone who has been camping understands, because this is why we go. Fire is hypnotic and uncages the imagination. As the night mellowed, we penned private thoughts in log books and discussed everything from the issues of 1979 to our favorite music. Hank pondered one peculiar mystery.

"Of all the people we've met on this trip, why is it that nobody has asked us to share a beer, but four have asked us to smoke a joint?" Just that day, the driver of the pickup who hitched us into Perley for groceries had become number four.

From the circle of knowledge, apostle Rich mellifluously replied, "So they can see some hills in this godforsaken flat."

May 18 began like any other day, but by dark it was well on its way to the bizarre. Pulling ashore for the night near a bridge, we set out to find the landowner, who happened to be walking to his truck parked by the road. As permanent envoy, I approached the stout young man who looked to be about our ages. Les was his name, and he quickly approved our stay on family land. He also mentioned that we could get a hot supper at a bar in Nielsville, a town of about a hundred residents just down the road. Returning to the canoes, I relayed the message that hot food was nearby. Our own style of celebratory dancing followed—which was more or less stomping the feet while raising one hand in the air, then the other. It wasn't a dance step that was likely to sweep the discos, or any sensible woman off her feet. But it was quite energetic, and showed our growing appreciation for food that didn't contain natural additives such as bug spit and wood ash.

Once camp was in order, we set off on the two-mile hike to Nielsville. Only a few hundred yards into it, a vehicle approached from behind and slowed. It was Les in his truck. We jumped into the back and headed to the bar, where Les immediately introduced us to his friends. Keith drew considerable attention in his Chiefs jacket— Morningside College, not the NFL team. A table of girls, who had probably never seen a guy so tall, assumed that he played for the pros—an assumption that we didn't actively refute. As Keith enjoyed his new football career, Les winked and whispered, "There ain't many girls around here, you know."

Les said he played basketball in high school, and after our tabletop pyramid of empty beer bottles reached Egyptian proportions, he hit upon a grand scheme. "Why don't you guys stick around for a couple of days? I'll line us up some games. We can whip anybody in Polk County."

I could see him salivate at the thought of walking onto the court with a towering center and two imposing power forwards. I was probably the free record they send you after ordering the nine-album set, although Les didn't make me feel that way. He talked as if we were all Olympic basketball veterans.

What happened after that is a bit fuzzy by all recollection. Closing down the bar, we somehow ended up in Les's hayloft, playing horse at a rusty basketball hoop until the morning birds sang. I'm not sure if this was intended to be the first scheduled practice for the upcoming county tour, but there we were, slipping on the loose hay, with Les nearly falling out an unlatched door to certain death onto a farm implement below. "You guys are good shits," Les kept repeating over and over. We felt the same about Les.

The exhibition tour was ultimately canceled, and we paid heavily for our nighttime antics. Daybreak came way too fast and brought rain with it. Drenched tents stuffed away, we skipped breakfast and set out in wretched drizzle, our heads aching from too much merriment and no sleep. Within a mile, it became obvious that we should have stayed put. By mid-afternoon, we could take no more punishment and opted for an early camp at the next available farm. A graying gentleman saw me coming through the yard and stepped out of the house to greet me. Cordial and well-spoken, he offered his farm: "Go ahead and camp. If you want, there's a shower in the barn."

Opening the "barn" door, I froze, mouth agape. This wasn't like any barn I had ever been in. In the middle of the huge pole building stood a mammoth combine, freshly washed, drying on the immaculately clean cement floor. One wall housed a complete metal workshop, hand tools so neatly organized that my father would have cried with joy to see them. (Whenever my brothers and I borrowed Dad's tools, he was happy if he ever saw them again.) In a room near the front of the building was a spotless full bathroom. Finishing my turn in the shower, I headed outside, feeling a little guilty for staying in the hot water for so long. Approaching the tents, I suddenly stopped. Something didn't look right.

"What's that?" I pointed.

"A casserole."

I shook the water out of my ears. "What?"

"I don't know. A guy just brought it out and asked if we were hungry."

The Bible says that pride leads to destruction, or something to that effect. Who were we to argue with providence? The casserole was delicious.

Shortly after devouring every scrap of food, we found ourselves inside the house, drinking iced tea with Gene and Margaret Sondreal. Nearing retirement, the Sondreals farmed more than a thousand acres, aided by several migrant workers who spent the summer in cottages near the main house. Both were genuinely excited about the trip, as were their hired hands who soon joined our little party. At one point, Gene sighed, "I thought about doing something like that once, but never did." In the brief silence that followed, it was clear he was searching to understand why he never went. This wasn't the first time we saw this struggle, nor would it be the last. Taking another deep breath, Gene came back to the present to tell us he had been to Manitoba. "I've done some fly-in fishing up near Lake Winnipeg. You can make it, but you have to be careful. That lake can be wild."

Sauntering back to the tents, we marveled at how supportive and trusting people had been with us. They seemed to be enamored with what we were doing, almost as if our journey was a lens for viewing their own daydreams. Until we reached Lake Winnipeg, our success relied on these river people. More than halfway there, we had been afforded nothing but kindness. Thanks to Gene and Margaret, the day went from dreadful to incredible in an instant. As we unzipped the tent flaps, something Les said the day before suddenly reemerged and made me smile: "It's a good thing you guys are camping on my land. I know where you are, in case somebody gets crazy with a gun." It hadn't crossed his mind that *we* might be the crazies.

In a quiet voice that belied his size, Keith sent us to bed with wisdom that would become a rallying cry during trying days to come.

"Pleasure is nothing without adversity's reflection." Aristotle couldn't have said it better.

∞

DAY 13. The river straightened for a bit, taking us a record twenty-five linear miles in one day. We rode that Autobahn all the way to Grand Forks. This stretch was mostly an uneventful paddle, except for a chance meeting with a couple of angels.

We had been plugging along, and barely noticed two small boys on the shore. As we passed them, a faint call floated across the water.

"You gonna shoot the dam?"

"Huh?" Our heads snapped forward, eyes scouring the water. The bright sun stared directly at us, making the water difficult to read, but everything seemed normal. With a shrug, we resumed our previous course.

Another muffled cry came from the shore. "You're going over the dam!" Quickly, we scanned the surface a second time, but again, didn't see anything unusual. Perhaps a check dam ahead was under high water, like the one back in Fargo. We figured we could slide right over it.

Moments later, my chest tightened and my hands got sweaty. Those kids seemed awfully excited about a dam that was submerged. "Maybe we should take a look," I petitioned.

It was time to get out of the canoes and stretch anyway, so we casually started for shore. As soon as we veered toward land, the dam instantly appeared (it's easier to see a change in elevation when looking at an angle to the river), and it *wasn't* under water. It *was* dead ahead and the distance was closing fast. "We gotta move!" Hank shouted, and we made a beeline for land, paddles whirring like airplane propellers.

Reaching the bank with only thirty feet to spare before the drop, we all exhaled deeply, nearly passing out with relief. Had we hit the dam, we would have capsized and been crushed against the cement, or jettisoned over the top. Undoubtedly, the boys saved us from a major disaster, and we spun around to thank them, but they were gone. Hank called out; nobody answered. The cherubs had vanished as quickly as they appeared. Somebody's guardian angels were looking after us that day.

Grand Forks was the third largest city on the route, surpassed only by Fargo and Winnipeg. Entering town just before nightfall, we paddled until coming to a park. The city was still reeling from high water, the park soggy and deserted. We weren't sure if camping was legal, or if the park was even open, but it was getting late. With no other options in sight, we committed our only known act of trespass. Waiting until after dark, we quietly pitched tents and moved in. First thing in the morning, we quickly tore down camp and slipped into the river. It was never clear whether any rules had been broken, but we told ourselves they had. Girls like outlaws.

North of Grand Forks, the river continued to be generous. Another unexpectedly straight stretch gave up twenty linear miles in five hours, so we knocked off early at Oslo, Minnesota. Indeed, the straight river was unanticipated because our only navigational chart was a common state road map, and by this point, we had learned not to bother asking residents what to expect up ahead. Most had never been on the water that separates Minnesota and North Dakota. This didn't always deter them from offering opinions though. On one occasion, a farmer informed us that, "Ya, the river is straight. You'll be to town in less than an hour." Three hours later, we were still paddling. Either the farmer had never paddled the Red, or he is still laughing.

Strolling into the village, we spied a deputy sheriff, casually leaning against his car. He was looking our way.

"Do you think he knows about Grand Forks?" someone whispered.

"Shhh! Be cool."

Unaware of the felons before him, the deputy made no arrests, and even pointed out public land near the river for a camp. A nice fellow, he punctuated every sentence with "Uff-da," a trademark of the local Scandinavian heritage. To celebrate this prosperous day of travel, the three fishermen went to try their luck for the elusive Atrazine catfish that Alan had described. Canned corn was the bait of choice—for the fishermen, but not the fish.

Rain cut the day short, so we settled in for a long evening at a restaurant in town. Our late night return trip included a lively discussion—about nuclear bombs. It all started with the realization that somewhere out in the lonely fields west of Grand Forks were silos containing intercontinental ballistic missiles. It then occurred to us that the silos, and we, were likely targeted by Soviet missiles. Not that the concept of being targeted was new. Anyone growing up in the sixties had done the "duck and cover" drill, that scenario intended to make kids believe that hiding under a desk would help. Our beef was whether we would get blown up before reaching Hudson Bay. That would really tick us off. A strange sight it must have been to see four scraggly canoeists walking along an empty, dark road, yelling at each other about whether man was dumb enough to destroy the world. No verdict was reached.

The river kept growing, but its width varied considerably, which made us wonder how steamboats had ever managed some of the tighter turns. Steamers first ran the river in 1859, but their zenith was the short decade from 1871 to 1880. This was after a railroad had been completed between Fargo and St. Paul, but before lines were driven to Winnipeg. A steamer captain would have to be vigilant. Catastrophe was around every corner, and there were a lot of corners.

At about this time in the trip, a routine developed that surprised all of us—regular paddling partners. In the beginning, we switched partners and boats daily, but over time, Hank and Rich settled in Lucky, and Keith and I became permanent fixtures in the Cad. Hank and Keith took up residence in the stern, Rich and I the bow. None of us remembers how this pattern came about. Maybe it was the best match of paddling styles, or maybe we just got lazy one day and never changed back. Certainly, the consistency made it much easier to position cargo so that the boats tracked smoothly. Some days, I missed being in the stern because I always felt at home there, but it was impossible to put Keith in front. No matter how much cargo we stuffed in the stern, the boat was always bow-heavy. We stuck with what worked best, and I came to appreciate the beauty of watching undisturbed water flow under us.

Having been out for two weeks, most of it on the tedious Red, even the simplest of amusements brought great joy. To entertain ourselves, we sometimes spoke of our progress in an Old English dialect. Okay, it was whatever a bunch of stir-crazy Iowa boys believed Old English *might* sound like, which was sort of a cross between Charles Dickens and Moses (who wasn't an Englishman, but had a great delivery).

"Ah, the river channel was a deceitful strumpet, but the young lads followed the true line, and it was good. And so it came to pass on their anointed and appointed journey to the border, and it was good."

Though we never saw such speech as anything more than just a little fun to pass the time, in a way, these stories were a sign that we were starting to take on a common identity. We were no longer just four guys sharing canoes. We were the Southland Lads, noble knights of the keel.

∞

ROUNDING A BEND one day, we came upon a dark shadow looming about fifteen feet up in a tree, wedged between two large limbs. It was much too big to be a squirrel nest. The trees were only just beginning to leaf out, so it wasn't an abnormally dense layer of leaves. Getting closer, the shape became familiar. It was a cow! Legend speaks of "cow tipping," the supposed weekend activity for bored Midwestern teens, but stashing them in trees? Nobody could be that bored. A little further downstream, we snapped a picture of a bale of hay, also in a tree, that must have been twenty feet above the water. Obviously the work of a recent massive flood, I shuddered at the thought of what must have taken place.

Floods on the Red River are infamous. Runoff from plowed farmland quickly fills the channel, and the spring thaw staggers from south to north, sending a steadily multiplying supply of water into frozen land that can't handle excess moisture. A late spring, like the current one, added to the trouble, delaying snow melt to coincide with the traditional time for heavier rain. Once it over-flows the bank, the Red can spread out for more than twenty miles across the flat countryside. Ever since we had entered the river, there had been signs of the reced-ing flood, but now we were in its last throes. The Orwell dam gatekeeper's words suddenly made sense—there was certainly "plenty of water." We were riding the tail of one of the largest Red River floods in recorded history.

It was hard to imagine that the meandering river could be so unruly and vicious, yet animal carcasses were snagged in the cabling under bridges and mired in the soggy shore. Road embankments displayed gaping holes that had been washed out or were filled with fresh shiny gravel. Although finding the river channel was sometimes challenging amid the floodwaters, we were occasionally able to bypass some of the wide and winding river bends by cutting across fields and through trees. At one point, we set the compass toward north, and just started paddling.

Many river residents and animals had not yet returned to their flooded homes, and a haunting stillness hung over the days, much as we imagined it would after the nuclear war of recent debate. Tiny tree buds harboring new life emerged in stark contrast to the desolate destruction. While in the midst of this wreckage, we spent a night next to a group of rural houses. Seeking out the landowner, we went from house to house, but not even a bird stirred. Peeking in the windows, we saw basements full of water, and bowls on the kitchen table, still filled with Corn Flakes. According to the map, we were camped by a bridge—that wasn't there. At the evening fire, we spoke softly, as if intruding upon something sacred or unnatural.

A particularly hard-hit area was Drayton, North Dakota, which had become a tiny island in a great sea. Three weeks earlier the river had crested at the highest level ever recorded in Drayton to that time, spilling into the fields for many miles. Even as we entered town, a two-mile-wide lake still surrounded the besieged community. On one side of a sweeping river bend, several houses stood watch over the retreating Red, safe for the moment, but not yet ready to trust the devious river. On the other side, bottomlands drowned under several feet of water. Pulling directly into the backyard of one house, we approached the occupants, who were standing outside, looking a little surprised that anyone would be brave or stupid enough to paddle down the unstable river. The landowners, Nick and Joyce, offered us whatever dry land was available. As we spoke, a neighbor and his boy started walking our way, the boy sprinting ahead to join the other kids gathering at the canoes. Every so often, we could see the children pointing and nodding, as if planning their own journey.

Later, Nick took us on a truck tour of the damage. It was bad, and what we saw was only a fraction of the peak flood. Nick drove us out past the sugar beet factory where he worked. It had survived, but Nick wasn't sure the crop season would fare so well. Despite the river's disruptions, Drayton endured. Teenagers cruised the streets in cars, just as they would any other humid summer night.

∞

THE LAST STOP before the Canadian border is Pembina, a sleepy village believed to be the first white settlement in North Dakota, and birthplace of important modifications to the Red River cart. These two-wheeled carts used no iron, were simple, durable, and easy to fix—the perfect tool for Métis wishing to circumvent the Hudson's Bay Company monopoly by transporting furs to St. Paul.

Showers were the first order of business, obtained via bargaining with a hotel manager. Groceries and laundry were next. Washing would never remove all the Red River muck and campfire soot, but everything would feel better. While waiting for the clothes to dry, I set out for the post office for stamps. As I walked, I contemplated the day's unsolved problem—finding a place to stay the night. A park near the river had been protected behind a sandbag levee during the flood, which kept the grounds in decent shape, but a sign said "No Tents." Once inside the post office, I explained our predicament to the postmaster. Squinting at me, he offered a solution.

"Stay in the park. If anyone asks you, tell 'em Johnny said it's okay. Nobody's been arrested yet in this town. Why should they start with you?"

We headed to the park, and tents quickly sprung up. As we worked, a police car came by. We went about our business with brass, hoping that confidence exuded innocence. Swinging around the park, the car crawled along, then stopped. Apparently, we didn't look confident enough. An officer got out, his long sigh suggesting that although we were not the first idiots he had dealt with, we might be the biggest ones. Staring at the two tents staked out not ten feet from the clearly printed "No Tents" sign, he took a deep breath and said politely, "There's no camping in the park."

Never having been arrested before, I was quick to the defense. "Johnny at the post office said it was okay." As I spoke, I realized how much I sounded like a six-year-old pleading a case to his mother for doing something he knew was wrong. Having entered "mother court" with stronger evidence than this, and lost, I knew our current position was weak.

The officer's lips narrowed, indicating that he really didn't think Johnny made the right call, or even possessed authority to make the call. But, much like a store that honors the price of a mismarked item, he relented. In a big city, we would have been booted, but this was a small town, where rules are subject to situational interpretation. After the officer heard the details of our quest, he seemed much more comfortable with the temporary zoning variance.

Later in the evening, I took a solitary walk around town. Setting my sights on the Tastee Freeze a few blocks away, I marveled at how much Pembina reminded me of home. Lined with several small businesses befitting a farm community, the main road funneled into a river bridge at one end, and headed off into the prairie at the other. Most importantly, it had an ice cream shop to cool the town folk after baseball games in the summer heat. While I savored a banana split, two high school girls who worked there asked questions about us (word travels fast in Pembina). Business was slow, so I spoke with Shelly and Lonna for quite a while. After two and a half weeks with the same three guys, it felt good to talk to other people, and if they happened to be cute girls, all the better. The girls extended an invitation to continue the conversation at Lonna's house after they closed shop.

Lonna's mom eyed me with all the intensity due a mother whose seventeen-year-old daughter brings home a transient college boy from the river, but she graciously accepted me into her home. While drinking a glass of lemonade, I spied an old guitar in the corner. Shelly asked me to play something. Things were going downhill fast for Mom, who now added rock 'n' roll to my list of dubious virtues. I think I saw her cringe as I picked up the Stella acoustic guitar, but her face immediately softened when I quietly played "Classical Gas," an instrumental piece from the tie-dyed generation. For the next half hour, the four of us talked and ate cookies.

My mind jumped about as I walked back to the park. Getting away from camp for a while had been refreshing, and I was excited about finally entering Canada, but Pembina also gave me a last glimpse of "home." I couldn't help but wonder if I would see it again.

CHAPTER 6

River Rats
and Renegades

OUR LAST MORNING in the states began with a hot breakfast and basketball. Turns out, a ten-year-old will rent his ball to strangers for a dollar. Who knew? As luck would have it, I turned my ankle on the edge of the cement ten minutes into the game. The kid got a good deal. Not even offering a prorated refund, the budding little capitalist was on his way to enslaving the proletariat.

Unless something was broken in there, I was familiar with what would follow. Having bowed legs that would make any cowboy jealous, I walk on the outside edges of my soles, making me susceptible to ankle injury. Bone fragments from numerous incidents testify to this. (One of those chips came during a high school basketball practice. As I lay screaming on the floor, the coach saw the angle at which my bowed leg leaves the knee, and asked if I was sure it was the ankle that hurt. I'm not positive, but I may have been a little disrespectful in my answer.) Given my history, one might question the wisdom of playing basketball in the first place, since a broken ankle would end the trip for all of us. Stupidity can be hard to defend.

With the ankle swelling quickly, we grabbed some ice from the girls at the Tastee Freeze, and I limped to the river. A surprise awaited us there. During the night, the flood had receded somewhat, leaving thirty feet of freshly exposed mud flat. Walking through the deep, slippery muck would be tricky. Even an uninjured person would find it difficult to carry heavy packs in such unstable conditions. Rich crossed the steel bridge in search of another route, but found it wasn't much better. The road bed was high and the channel cut deep, leaving behind a steep greasy slope covered with brush. Rich was able to pick his way down to the water, but getting the canoes and gear through the tangle was a different story. Besides, the night before we had purposefully left our canoes at the water's edge back on the other side to avoid a similar slope there. It didn't make sense to pull them all the way up, just to cross the bridge and fight our way back down.

After some thought, an alternative plan was hatched. Two guys would brave the mud, and drag the empty canoes to the water's edge. The other two would then lower the gear by rope from the bridge. Once loaded, the mudders would paddle to the other side and meet the remaining two passengers. Being injured, I was exempted from the "rock, paper, scissors" that decided mud duty.

Keith won, and took up a position with me on the bridge. Rich and Hank struggled in the gunk, using the boats for balance. Laughing in the beginning, but cussing by the end, they moved slowly forward. From the bridge, Keith and I only joined in the laughing, glad that it was them, and not us.

Meanwhile, an old man in coveralls and a red seed corn hat came to the river bank carrying a Polaroid camera. Assuming he was going to give us a snapshot for posterity, I asked why he was taking a picture.

"The guys back in the bar won't believe this," he explained.

Dumbfounded, we laughed even harder. He walked off, picture in hand.

Later, as we floated downstream, Hank and Rich dangled their mud-caked shoes and legs over the gunwale. It may have been the first time anyone ever used the silty Red to wash anything. Clean is relative.

Halfway through the third week, we had finally reached the border. Taking a short break to celebrate the occasion with a cheap bottle of wine purchased in Pembina, we coasted onto shore and hiked to a highway that followed the river. We needed to clear our entry at a checkpoint. Walking was slow on an ankle decorated with a new purple splotch, but the ice had helped hold the swelling down, and I found a piece of driftwood to use as a crutch. Not accustomed to pedestrians, the border guards were visibly uneasy as four unshaven young males approached on foot—three of them giants, and one with a big stick. I thought, "Great. All the way to Canada, and I get shot at the border."

When they heard our story, skepticism replaced the guards' apprehension. It was their job to be suspicious, and I doubt that our profile was included in the customs manual. They may have thought we were running drugs— all of the pot those flatlanders wanted to share had to come from somewhere. The questions are the same for everyone entering the country, but they suddenly seemed directed specifically at us.

"How long are you planning to stay in Canada?"

"We don't know. Maybe a couple of months." That was vague. Strike one.

"Do you have any alcohol?"

"A little wine and whiskey." Strike two. I wondered what Canadian jail was like.

"Do you have any firearms?"

Now, we were in big trouble, because we had changed our minds and came armed. "We have a Wrist Rocket slingshot."

The guards choked to contain their laughter as they realized they were looking upon backcountry greenhorns, bound to never return.

"Do you want to come down and look in the canoes?" we invited.

Briefly calculating the distance to the river, one guard looked out the window at the line of cars waiting their turns for inspection, then raised an eyebrow toward his buddy. "Good luck, eh."

It was official. We were canoeing Canadian waters. Although we were on the same river we had been paddling forever, it felt different now. The sun was shining, it was warm outside, and the river seemed straighter. Even a strong headwind didn't bother us—it was a Canadian wind.

∞

"INCREDIBLE." IN LETTERS that crossed an entire page, I penned the opening to my first Canadian journal entry. Crossing the border was a landmark, but proved to be only the beginning of a series of events that Keith would later summarize as "Stuff That Changed History."

It all began with a stop for water and a place to camp. On shore, we met Diny Houle and his sister, Carole, who were tending the family dairy herd. Diny was about twenty years old, slim, wore glasses, and spoke with the French Canadian accent that dominates many small villages in southern Manitoba. Because of the flood, water from the farm well wasn't safe to drink, but Diny gladly shared their drinking water supply, which they replenished daily from nearby Letellier.

On his way to the barn for evening chores, Diny stopped by our campsite to meet everyone, and surprised us with an offer. "You guys want to go to a wedding social?"

We all shrugged. "What's a social?"

"It's one big drunk. I'll come back in an hour or two and get you."

"We're pretty dirty." "We don't really have any nice clothes." "We don't know anyone!" We all piped up at once.

"Don't worry, eh. Wash up in the house." Not waiting for a reply, Diny headed off into the barn. Trusting fellows, these Canadians.

Despite our lack of proper attire, we had taken this trip to see the world. What better way than to join in a traditional local festivity? We scrubbed up the best we could, dressing in the clothes with the cleanest dirt. Our destination was an unpretentious community hall in the little village of St. Jean Baptiste. A wedding social turned out to be a wedding reception in reverse. People from up and down the river converged on the hall, overflowed into the parking lot, and drank and danced for hours. This was familiar, not unlike a wedding bash in the states. However, the couple had not yet been married. Attendees celebrated and gave money to the couple *before* the wedding, instead of after. (We Americans like to see some proof of the hitchin' before we hand over cash.)

While kids dashed about and a seventy-year-old couple boogied to the *Saturday Night Fever* soundtrack, Diny introduced us to his friends. "Look at the river rats and renegades I found."

We were immediately befriended and felt at home. It was Keith's birthday, and someone asked the emcee to announce the occasion, and our trip. Both got cheers and some puzzled looks. We contributed to the wedding pot and met the prospective bride and groom. She looked radiant, as all future brides do. He looked worried.

Later in the night, we moved to Pete and Paulette's house, where we played pool in the basement and talked until early morning. Stretched out on two stools in a corner, I occasionally chatted, but mostly watched quietly. The French language lilted in comparison to the familiar rigid English. This was especially true when the girls spoke. TV had taught us about French women. They were always dark haired, beautiful, and playfully seductive. We found no evidence to contradict this.

There was something unique about this group. Having fun was paramount to living, yet underneath the carefree exterior was an unusual bond. Each member constantly looked out for the others, with honesty and candidness that was unfamiliar to us. Nothing was hidden, no subject off limits. They treated us the same way, but it took a while for us to open up and reciprocate. I first experienced this when Diny asked me what I thought of the U.S. oil crisis. Having grown up during years when the phrase "we're out of gas" wasn't always a teenage ploy to initiate necking, I certainly had views on the subject. But, unsure of our hosts' perspective, I answered as if running for political office. Diny nodded at my senatorial speech, then offered a more concise and sincere appraisal.

"I suppose we'll bail you Americans out, eh? If we don't give you oil, I suppose you'll come up here and take it. Boy, will I write you a nasty letter."

And I believed he would.

Later in the evening, this honesty let us in on a little secret. Hank was lauding the great trust the Houles had shown us, when from across the room, Diny hooted. "Eh, what you didn't see was that I loaded the gun and carried it to the barn with me. And I figured I could keep an eye on you at the social, where we outnumbered you!"

So, the initial level of trust was a little shaky. He deserved credit for thorough planning.

We had such a good time hanging out that we stayed another day. Our new friends introduced us to several local delicacies at Barney's, a drive-in restaurant. We indulged in pizza pops, potato and cheese pierogies, and vinegar chips. Chips are french fries to us, but Belgian fries to the French (don't ask me). Someone quickly arranged an afternoon gathering at a park, the stated purpose of which was to celebrate Keith's birthday, although I think any excuse for a party would have sufficed. Either way, I was glad for the day off, because I could barely walk.

Twenty-five young people joined us to relax on a beautiful day. Sometime in the afternoon, a game of Canadian-style basketball got under way. From a grassy courtside seat, I noticed that the northern rules incorporated several aspects of hockey. Body-checking was legal, and dribbling was somewhat optional. Pal, a lovable local hockey icon, shone in this rendition of the game. According to legend, he had spent forty-two minutes of one hockey game in the penalty box. Fable or not, if Pal went up against Wilt Chamberlain in Canadian hoops, I'd give him even odds.

From a plowed field next to the park came a high-pitched "Yoooooooo." That was Satch.

Karl and Beef responded in kind, triggering a chorus of Yooooooos that indicated the discovery of another worm. A hunting expedition had been organized to gather fish bait for the evening campfire at Diny's.

There, a smaller gathering continued with the same group of friends as the night before. Activities varied, depending upon personal interests. Pal jousted with a tree to a draw. Keith, whose college specialty was natural science, helped Diny's sister study the components of the human eye for a biology test. Hank noted that Keith had probably celebrated his birthday with enough gusto to be questionable as the American emissary of education, but Carole seemed bright, and I anticipated that she would double-check her new professor's guidance.

As the group slowly dwindled, I made one last journal entry for the day. "Just like the license plate says, 'Friendly Manitoba'."

∞

IT WAS HARD to leave in the morning, but we had to push on. Winnipeg, the end of our first leg, was just two days out. Located at the "forks," where the Assiniboine River meets the Red, Winnipeg was a natural crossroads, first for indigenous peoples, and later for Hudson's Bay Company. To us, Winnipeg was a contradiction. Several times the population of Fargo, it was within a few days paddling of unspoiled paradise.

At the final camp before reaching the city, an unexpected opportunity to hone our survival skills arose. Keith spotted a rabbit in the bushes, and with visions of roasted meat stirring his imagination, he quietly grabbed the Wrist Rocket from the top of the pack. Realizing that the steel marbles were buried somewhere deep in the pack, he looked around for alternative ammunition. Rocks were scarce, but Hank, with wisdom born of a lifetime of aiding his little brother, reached for the tiny transistor radio he had brought, opened the back plate, pulled out the nine-volt battery, and handed it to Keith. Keith cautiously studied the ammo for a second, but with time running short, he pulled back the sling, took aim, and let go. In a classic Bugs Bunny and Elmer Fudd moment, the battery struck his hand, and whirred as it flip-flopped up into the air, peacefully coming to rest a few feet from the rabbit. The creature turned to assess the danger posed by wayward batteries falling from the sky, then casually hopped away. It took a moment for Keith to feel the pain of his traumatized wrist, but when he did, he let out a howl. Just below the thumb, two inches of skin had been laid back. As we did our best to patch him up, we tried not to crack too many jokes about his hunting prowess. He was smarting enough without our help. Of course, our respect was only temporary. Soon we were assailing him with remarks such as, "What size battery do you prefer for squirrels?"

A cold drizzle pelted us all the way to Winnipeg, soaking our bodies and dispositions. Before lunchtime, the day had already been nominated for immediate placement onto Keith's list for "adversity's reflection." Numbing as cold drizzle is, our cheap, unbreathable rain gear amplified the condition, causing us to sweat and freeze at the same time. Even the sound of the rain became maddening, droplets plunking on our hoods with the repetitive tick of a clock on the last day of school.

The rain on that day wouldn't raise the river level much, but Winnipeg prepared for worse. Just outside the city is a flood control project known as Duff's Ditch, a huge trench dug around one side of Winnipeg. A dam can be closed during high water, diverting part of the river around the city to a point many miles away, where it rejoins the Red. The scale is immense. More earth was excavated to dig this trench than was moved for either the Panama Canal or the Suez Canal. Quite an odd spectacle, the project testified to the power that an angry Red River could unleash.

Needing some stimulation on the dreary day, we raced for the dam. Keith and I had the faster boat, but Rich and Hank hung in there, until Rich's paddle broke. The paddle was possibly flawed, although Rich maintained that no paddle could withstand his mighty "guns," which he flexed for our benefit. Keith and I dismissed the trash talk, but nobody ignored the lesson learned—no racing. Paddles weren't easily replaced in the bush.

It had taken three weeks to get to Winnipeg. Originally, we had planned to stay at a park for a few days while making final preparations for the next legs, but it was such a foul day that we stashed the canoes under a highway bridge, sought the cheapest hotel in the area, and moved there. I steamed in a hot bath for an hour.

The hotel turned out to be a good idea, because in the morning we learned that the campground was still closed from the flood, and wasn't conveniently located anyway. Rooms weren't in the budget, so we searched for still cheaper accommodations. They don't really make hotels cheaper than the one we were at, but by chance, we found a manager who took great interest in our quest, and he cut us a good rate. His hotel was just down the road, so the move there wasn't more than a medium portage.

One thing that didn't come with our rooms was parking space for the canoes, which were still tucked under the bridge. It was critical that we find a safe place quickly, because footprints under the bridge indicated that someone had already taken one boat out for a joyride. The joy-rider had kindly returned the canoe unharmed, but our vessels were too important to leave unattended. The next time someone borrowed one, it might be a one-way trip. A call to the Winnipeg Canoe Club solved the problem.

The historic club generously extended the use of its warehouse. All we had to do was paddle there, and take a taxi back. A peek inside the club warehouse revealed watercraft of all kinds, from knife-like rowing sculls to a huge war canoe. We tried to hide our envy for the elegant wooden boats, not wishing to offend the plain-looking aluminum canoes that had brought us so far. The rowing coach who led us on a tour of the facility remarked that our trip should be exciting. Like everyone else, he warned against taking risks on Lake Winnipeg.

For the next few days, we split time between loafing, locating maps, sight-seeing, renting a short-wave communications radio, and hiring someone for the return air pickup from Hudson Bay. Concerns began to emerge about our air agent, who didn't have a good reputation with some of the companies he represented. I was all for making a last-minute agent switch, but we went with our original contact. I prayed that he paid our pilot in advance.

A short-wave radio was needed to call for a plane to come get us. A single caretaker still lived at York Factory, or so we were told, but we weren't sure there would be access to a wireless. Short-wave radios were not always reliable, being susceptible to changing atmospheric conditions, but it was either that or set a predetermined pickup date. Not knowing how many weeks it would take us to get there, an arranged date was a shaky guess at best. Perhaps even more significant, setting a date would make us slaves to a schedule, which went against our every reason for going. Radios weren't cheap. Rental ate up four hundred dollars of our budget, but the freedom to travel at our own pace was deemed worth the cost.

During one of our more interesting outings, to a natural history museum, we learned about the wildlife farther north. Countless displays painted a picture of what lay ahead. Rounding a corner, I saw the others intently staring at an exhibit.

"Weeee doggies."

"That is one big mama."

"Ho-ly cow."

Curious, I peeked in their direction. When I caught sight of the display, my spine turned to liquid. It was a stuffed polar bear. Looking at the giant, I understood what it felt like to be somewhere below the top of the food chain. It was humbling, but edifying. Staring into the bear's dark eyes, I felt foolishly arrogant, and hopeful that those who see arrogance are less the fools of it.

The display was a female bear, considerably smaller than a twelve hundred-pound male. They got bigger than this? It could outrun us, swim as fast as we could paddle, and eat hundred-and-fifty-pound seals for snacks. I weighed in at only a hundred and thirty pounds, so I wasn't even a good appetizer. I looked at the three big shaggy Iowa seals standing next to me. Maybe a bear would prefer the full-course meal.

Bears weren't the only hungry mammals. Eating became a main pastime, and we stuffed ourselves at every opportunity. Across the street from the hotel was an all-you-can-eat buffet that we shamefully destroyed on our first afternoon in town. That is, it *was* all-you-can-eat until we returned the next day. Next to the plates was a freshly penciled sign informing patrons that each subsequent trip to the buffet would cost another dollar. The looks cast at us from the waitstaff suggested that a strong connection existed between our appetites the previous day and the additional charge. We politely paid the extra dollar, then piled food on the plate as high as it would go without toppling.

Cultural differences with our neighbors to the north were mostly minor, but one nearly got me killed. Returning to the hotel from a food run, I cautiously approached a busy six-lane boulevard. There was no stoplight, just a worn crosswalk painted on the pavement. Back home, crosswalk markings are just pretty pictures to enjoy. In the states, successful fording of an automotive river of this magnitude required the speed of a white-tailed deer. It's our way of thinning the herd. Too slow, and splat. Too timid, and you starve. I stretched my legs to loosen up in preparation for the mad dash. As cars whizzed by, I tried to remember my physics. "Acceleration equals mass times something. No, it is mass divided by something . . ."

Intent on my calculations, I didn't notice that the cars weren't zooming by. I looked up to see all lanes on my side of the boulevard at a standstill, drivers eyeing me intently. Like a racoon in headlights, I danced from foot to foot, unsure what to do. I wanted to believe the gesture was sincere, but what if they were just toying with an unsuspecting foreigner? I saw the drivers' impatience growing, so I took a step. I thought I saw a car inch forward, and I froze again. One driver shook her head and mouthed a few words, but didn't move. It must be a law! I darted across, not turning to see if I got the Canadian finger, which I assume is the same—except maybe a little shorter once the exchange rate has been applied. Reaching the safety of the center median, cars in the other lanes magically stopped, and this time I strolled across as if I flew the Maple Leaf.

Toward the end of our stay in the city, we spent an evening with some of the Letellier clan, who had come to Winnipeg for a birthday social. Birthday socials adhere to a peculiar custom of giving one "bumps." Guests grab hold of a large blanket and throw the birthday honoree high into the air, trampoline-style. It looked like fun, but seemed best done early in the night, while the throwers are still sober.

Although time spent in Winnipeg was a welcomed break, the urge to be off was strong once preparations were in order. Pulling away from the Canoe Club dock, we dug our lonely paddles deep into the water, letting the river welcome us back into her arms. Wilderness wasn't far away.

CHAPTER 7

The Witch
of Winnipeg

LAKE WINNIPEG SITS just forty miles north of the city, shielded by two final obstacles—the St. Andrews dam at Lockport and the Red River delta. Until the dam and lock were completed in 1910, the St. Andrews rapids were natural barriers to boat traffic. Ships could come down to the rapids from Winnipeg, but no further. Once completed, the lock gave boats direct access to Lake Winnipeg from anywhere on the Red River.

We hit the dam on the first day and spent the night on a long peninsula that extended upstream from the outer wall of the lock. Created when an approach canal was dug to the lock, the peninsula funneled boats into a safe channel. Spanning the two hundred-yard-wide river were several columns supporting a road above. Movable metal plates that were wedged between the pilings kept the water deep enough to feed the lock, and could be adjusted to allow ice jams to pass. Compared to the youthful stream back at Breckenridge, this river was an adult. From a grassy knoll on the peninsula, we could feel its beguiling power and the dam's feeble attempt to subdue it.

An evening outing on the mainland revealed two dozen fishermen staking out positions on a cement pier below the dam. Modern anglers found good luck there, just as ancient fishermen had found good luck at the rapids. One small boy who had tired of fishing wandered off, intent on retrieving the last crumbs from a bag of potato chips. Nearby, his father calmly fished with one eye on the river and one on his nomadic son. A child's spirit is no more tameable than a river.

The enormous lock opened to most boats, including canoes. Two huge steel doors at each end of a cement chamber closed, then the chamber was flooded or drained to raise and lower boats. Ingeniously, gravity did most of the work. It sounded like overkill for our tiny vessels, until we plotted the portage required to go around fences and over the raised road. Fortunately, the facility began its operating season the next morning, at which time we claimed first-of-year honors, much to the chagrin of a motorboat waiting on the other side. Going in the lock wasn't bad, but as the water level dropped several feet, the welling surface hinted at the chaos below, and we nervously clutched the safety ropes. The lock operator casually sat on the brim of the concrete hole, dangling his legs over the edge while monitoring the progress. A handful of anglers and a flock of white pelicans greeted our exit. From here on, our waters flowed free.

∽

AS THE RED RIVER entered the delta, it began to veer off in all directions. Encompassing fifty square miles, the delta is a confusing mass of interconnected channels and shallow lakes. Land and water meld together, creating a surreal maze that blurs liquid and solid. Well into the unearthly jumble, we encountered a strange phenomenon that added to the mystique—large waves that seemed to exist for no reason. They remained stationary, as if downstream from a big rock, but no upstream obstacle caused the disturbance. Confronted with this oddity, Hank remembered something he had once read in a magazine. On very large lakes, wind can push the water to one end, piling it up. Once the wind stops, the water retreats and starts a very slow sloshing motion, like when you step out of a bathtub. These motions are called seiches, and they can create substantial water surges and retreats.

Was this an incoming Lake Winnipeg seiche fighting with the outgoing river? Hank's premise had merit. Blustery winds had ruled for two days, and we figured that the shallows of the delta would be a prime battleground between river and surge. The wave hypothesis was never resolved, but seemed plausible and was probably more credible than two other popular theories—aliens, or Aquaman. Of course, this theory implied that the lake must be awfully big. I preferred the little green men.

Approaching storms caught us in the delta, surrounded by marsh that stretched beyond sight. We hadn't seen solid ground for some time and didn't know how far it was to the lake, so when a small oasis of stunted trees appeared, we called it a day. Barely a foot above water, the tiny island of gnarled shrubs was short on firewood and long on skunk, whose scent regularly wafted into camp. I don't know how the critter got there, but it was never more than forty feet away, because neither was the river. With nothing else to do, we spent the night in a fierce competition of Crazy Eights. The loser of each card game had to fetch another stick for the fire, braving wet feet and skunk. With so much incentive to deal from the bottom of the deck, we watched each other like gunfighters playing poker in an Old West saloon.

Cloaked in ghostly darkness by night, the marsh came to life by day. As we headed away from the little island, an early morning sun shimmered on the rippling water, ducks splashed about, and gulls floated overhead. Brown fields of reeds swayed peacefully in a light breeze. Our anticipation grew when the channel widened, and then there it was, the lake of bad temperament, deceptively calm. To the left and right, the shoreline arced away to form a huge U-shaped bay, each coast dissolving into a dashed line as the curvature of the earth carried the trees below the horizon. Straight ahead, the lake was one with the sky. I turned to Keith, whose mouth was open, but no words were coming out. Finally, he managed to speak. "*What* were we thinking?"

Three hundred miles of lake loomed before us. What *were* we thinking, indeed.

It was a good thing we stopped when we did the night before, because "skunk island" turned out to be the only dry spot in the rest of the delta. Once on the lake, our plan was simple—paddle whenever possible for as long as possible. There would be no dallying on this leg of the trip. We had heard too many stories about how quickly Lake Winnipeg could change, and how weather could stay bad for a week. How long it would take to conquer our three hundred-mile crossing was a source of friendly dispute. Hank thought it might be possible to get sixty miles on a good day, but I thought maybe closer to forty (based on twelve hours a day at three and a half miles per hour in good paddling conditions). We made a bet: If we were off the lake in ten days or less, I would buy everyone a beer when we arrived at Norway House, assuming there was beer to be bought. If it took longer, Hank would buy. Ten days meant averaging thirty miles per day, even on days lost due to poor weather. More than two days spent weathered in on shore would probably be enough to protect my wallet. The bookies in Las Vegas would give me good odds. The race was on.

Moving up the eastern shore, we spied cabins nestled between trees atop a short bluff. The unimpeded views from up there must have been striking. It would take a day to get clear of the cabins and beaches that offered escape to Winnipeg residents seeking refuge during the summer. Once past this little strip of civilization, the eastern shore quickly turned wild, surrounded by endless forests and swamps. A couple of tiny settlements were accessible by boat and plane, but there was little else.

Weather was our biggest concern on Lake Winnipeg, but that first day on the lake was filled with sun and light seas lapping at us from the side. As evening drew near, the wind died completely, turning the surface of the lake to glass. Except for subtle oceanlike heaving, the water was still. Stopping only long enough to cook supper, we paddled on, taking advantage of good fortune. Looking out across the lake, I could see the other canoe gliding alongside ours, silhouetted against a deep yellow fireball that hung low in a cloudless horizon. This was what we had come for.

Midnight approached and we were still going strong. The sun had set two hours ago, but the skyline glowed and the moon was bright. I didn't think it was possible to beat the day we had, but canoeing by moonlight did. The serenity was indescribable.

At Victoria Beach, a crucial decision had to be made. Hank spread out the map, turned on a flashlight, and outlined the situation.

"We're on a long point, at the tip of Traverse Bay. The safe route is to follow the shore down into the bay. That'll take an entire day. The more direct route is to cut straight across, a voyage of six miles on open water."

I guessed everyone was thinking the same thing I was. Conditions were ideal for taking such a risk, but the unusually long winter that year had postponed summer—a person would last only fifteen minutes in the freezing water. Many people had cautioned us that the lake could change in an instant, not to mention that it was after midnight, and we had seen only one other boat all day. A vote was in order.

Rich cast the first ballot. "Hmmm."

Hank followed. "Beats me."

Keith. "Geez, I don't know."

I added a final, "Uhhh . . ."

There you have it. Democracy at its finest.

Unanimous indecisiveness led to a less complex decision matrix. Rich flipped the coin. Across the bay it was!

The other side of the bay wasn't actually visible in the dimming light, so we picked a spot on the map, set the compass, and lined up a star to follow. The star would move in the sky during the crossing, but we figured we would be close enough for the two-hour paddle. Devil Island was the intended target, just off the opposite shore. I thought it appropriate that our destination was named after the big kahuna of temptation. Was he baiting us with a shortcut? Slipping into the blackness, I couldn't help but wonder if *this* was the foolish gamble that everyone had warned us to avoid.

An hour into the crossing, stars that had been clearly reflected in the calm water began to dance as a gentle wind scratched at the surface. Nobody spoke, but I heard the trickling of water from the bow change to a steady swoosh, indicating an increase in speed—we were paddling as fast as we could. Luck was again our friend, as the winds never picked up, and at two in the morning, we hit the island, just as hoped, er, planned. We weren't sure that it was the right island, but it was an island, and that was good enough. Great boasting and celebration accompanied this navigational success, so much that we barely noticed that the surface of the island was moving, crawling, alive. A flashlight revealed hundreds of nesting terns. This island was a rookery! It took a few minutes, but we managed to find another island that hadn't already been spoken for.

∞

THE NEXT MORNING, a shrill "Ayyyyyyy" shattered the tranquility. I jumped up and ran down to the water, expecting to see Keith lying on the rocks with a broken leg. He had gone to bathe in the lake, and I figured he must have slipped. Instead, I saw the big guy jumping around naked, rubbing himself with a towel so fast that I thought he would ignite. Apparently, the water was a bit cold. I was next, and suddenly bath time didn't summon the same enchanting memories as my toy submarine and

Mr. Bubble. I made the mistake of sticking a foot in first. What depravity forces us to touch the fire, even though we know it is hot? Taking a deep breath, I let out a similar whoop and ran in up to my knees. I splashed about for thirty seconds, whooped again, and was back up on the rocks in under a minute, trying to light a fire of my own.

Canoe travelers on Lake Winnipeg must learn to ride waves, and by our second day on the lake, wave class was underway. At first, it was unnerving to feel the canoe rise on the swells and to look back down into the deep troughs. Once accustomed to the vertical lifts, though, we took advantage of waves moving parallel to us, paddling to stay on the downslope as long as possible. There was no sense wasting energy on the upslope of a passing wave, so we stutter-paddled; hard strokes on the downslope, easy strokes on the upslope.

Waves coming broadside tested our nerve, and took some time to master. Our first instinct was to rigidly fight the natural roll of the boat—the opposite of what you should do. We eventually learned that fluid hips allow the boat to rock safely over a wave while the torso remains stationary, much like a snow skier on a mogul run. Captained by roll veterans, a canoe can handle surprisingly big water, as long as the waves aren't breaking. Breaking waves can bury a boat in a random wall of water, or smash headlong into the side, jolting occupants overboard. Though broadside waves were scary, diagonal ones were the most unpredictable, and often exhausting. Each wave twisted the canoes sideways, causing instability and forcing us to constantly steer back on course. Depending on the angle of the coastline, sometimes it was easier to zigzag through diagonal waves, going with them for a while, then turning to run directly broadside. The zigzag course was a little longer, but safer and less fatiguing.

Each type of wave has a certain feel, and after a while, we could ride them with our eyes closed. Our budget outriggers, purchased exclusively for use on Lake Winnipeg, proved to be more nuisance than beneficial. Consisting of foam tubes attached to short aluminum poles clamped perpendicular to the gunwales, they caught the water during rolls, slowing the boat and jarring us off balance. It wasn't long before we reversed the tubes, and mounted them on the topside of the poles, out of the way.

Hidden shoals pepper the coast of Lake Winnipeg, their threat dependent on lake conditions. In flat water, they caused only moderate concern for our canoes; catching a rock straight on the bow would put pressure on the strongest part of the boat, and the momentum would be directed along a straight line, reducing the likelihood of overturning. However, in heavy seas we were at danger of being driven into rocks with greater force, and at odd angles. Large waves also make it extremely difficult to right a flipped canoe, and in cold water that quickly saps energy and impairs thinking, the survival clock runs fast.

One of the most treacherous shoals is at Observation Point, where a line of barely submerged boulders extends nearly a mile into the lake. The hazard has been well documented, having taken its toll for centuries, yet it still almost got us. Normally, we rarely strayed more than several hundred yards from shore, but close to the point, we started moving out. Assuming we were clear of the shoal, we began riding the waves that were headed northeast. A few minutes later, a splash off the starboard side caught our attention. It didn't look right. It wasn't. In seconds, a boulder surfaced from beneath a swell, charging upward fast. We had misjudged the distance, just as countless others have. And, just as previous travelers have caught a favorable wave that took them over the rocks, so did we. Both of our canoes were carried over with only a slight bump.

Civilization quickly faded behind us. The lake was ours, and we were awestruck daily. The boundless sky revealed cloud patterns that weren't visible on a smaller horizon. It was as if we had always viewed clouds through binoculars, and were seeing the full picture for the first time. Never-ending coastline was undisturbed by man's hands nor noisy machines. Stony islands dotted the shore, and as at Devil Island, many were rookeries. Each kind of bird took over its own island. The terns owned one, the gulls another, and the cormorants yet another.

At about this point in time, we ate our first fish of the trip, two sheepshead caught in the mouth of a river. Some of the crew maintained that they were good eatin'. I don't remember, so either they were okay, or so bad that I have blocked out the memory.

Intoxicated by its magnificent beauty, we began to think that the lake had unfairly been given a bad rap. It didn't seem so bad, so we continued with a bold attack. One day, in order to avoid navigating a deep bay, we decided to cut some time with a two-mile jump to Black Island. Once there, we planned to follow the large island as it angled back toward the shore we were following. The day was sunny and calm, and we had already made a similar crossing that morning.

We were halfway across, laughing at Rich's norske impression—which sounded a lot like the Swedish Chef from the Muppets—when from behind me, I felt Keith stop paddling. From across the way, Hank and Rich did the same. "Do you hear that?" Hank asked, suddenly serious.

Laying the paddle across my lap, I listened. From the island came a steady *whishing* noise, like an idling steam engine. I saw nothing, but within moments, the locomotive went from idle to full throttle, advancing fast. "What is it?" I asked, nervously.

Toward the island, the water changed from shiny light blue to ruffled deep cobalt, and we knew. "It's the wind!"

The first wall of air hit us like a sinister eddy, the kind that often preceded an explosive thunderstorm. After the initial blast, a momentary lull ensued, and then the wind began steadily increasing. Within a minute, it was howling in our ears. Within two, it was thumping them like a bass drum. Waves whipped up rapidly, and broke over our bows. Inside the canoes, water accumulated fast. The extra weight slowed our progress—a snail's pace, into the wind—and plowed us still deeper into the swells. It was impossible to bail because it took both people paddling hard just to keep the boats straight. A vicious downward cycle developed as heavy boats took on more water, making them even heavier. The fierce wind drove the spray horizontally, every droplet pecking at our faces. We bellowed words of encouragement, only to have them swallowed in the deafening din. Each of us felt alone.

In the first minutes of the storm, we had an opportunity to turn around and take a chance with the rocks back on the mainland. But the direction of the wind would have driven us across a bay, giving the waves a longer distance to develop; regardless, that opening was long past. To turn broadside now would be too risky, even for a moment. In this frigid and tempestuous water, a flipped canoe was a death sentence.

I pulled with vengeance, cussing the lake each time. Not an avid cusser, I quickly ran out of words, but I think I made my point. For half an hour we fought the lake for our lives, and it was winning. The island was just ahead, but it seemed just ahead for a long, long time. I saw Hank and Rich struggling alongside, when from the rear seat came a voice that sounded like it was a hundred yards behind me. "Den! I think we're getting closer. *Pull!*"

With a deep breath and one last curse about the lake's family tree, I dug in as hard as I could. Nearing exhaustion, we fought to enter the protected lee side of the island. I could feel the wind release its grip on us, and heard it laugh in a haughty voice that trailed into the sky, "Haaaa ha ha ha ha."

Compared to the froth behind us, the calm was spooky. Waterlogged boats rode low in the water and ground to a halt on the gravel bottom, short of the shore. After emptying our cargo and laying everything out to dry, we collapsed on the flat boulders, soaking up the affections of the sun goddess—so unlike her wicked twin sister, the wind witch. There were congratulations at successfully skirting death again, but they were soft. We had won, but we knew that the lake had let us. Like the top-ranked high school tennis player who once toyed with me on the court for the amusement of his girlfriend, the lake had toyed with us, probably for the amusement of Lake Manitoba, that cute little thing just to the west. Winnipeg could give us a sporting chance, or trounce us at will. It just wanted to make sure we were aware of this.

Lying on my back, eyes closed, I heard a quiet utterance from a nearby rock. "What a nasty, nasty lake."

From a different rock, I heard another voice. "Don't cuss the lake."

The second voice was right. Today had been a tantrum. What if it got really mad? We apologized. Nobody ever cussed Lake Winnipeg again.

CHAPTER 8

Riding the Tiger

JOURNAL ENTRY, June 11:

> "OH MAN!! Fifty miles. A glorious calm day and we
> took advantage of it. Very cold night and up at 5:00.
> Paddled fourteen hours to Princess Harbour—maybe
> ten tiny houses, and a wireless transmitter connected
> to an old phone booth in a small clearing. Went
> around the point and stayed at a real nice camp."

Our fifty-mile day was filled with contradictions. On
one hand, it was a source of pride at the accomplishment.
On the other, it was tedious and exhausting. Late in the
afternoon, Keith and I were in the lead canoe and stopped
for a drink. Hank and Rich came up from behind, and
I grabbed the camera and a small telephoto lens that my
brother had loaned me. Zooming in, I could clearly see
the regular cadence of paddles slicing the water, and the
weary faces behind each stroke. That picture tells the
truth; ninety-five percent of any adventure is spent in

daily drudgery. Yet, most people who have viewed that photo haven't really *seen* it. They want spectacular landscapes, perils, or funny stories, and quickly move on to the next picture. It is drudgery they have, and adventure they seek.

Just before Princess Harbour, the lake is dramatically pinched, nearly creating two separate bodies. The upper part is the largest, a hundred and eighty miles long and sixty miles across. Despite its great size, Lake Winnipeg isn't terribly deep in most spots, but as my non-floating friend Dave says, "If it's over my head, what's the difference?" Dave makes sense, but strangely, there is some psychological difference between fifty feet of water and five hundred.

Making our way up the lake, we continued to paddle hard, but were properly respectful when the lake said "no." Our progress was good, though the lake continued to provide glimpses of its volatile reputation. The wind would blow for half a day, then suddenly let up. Two hours later, it would again come screaming across the water, chasing us off. A spectacular sunset might cap off the day, but by midnight, a thunderstorm could be slashing at the tents. Rich became our weatherman, exhibiting an uncanny ability to sense approaching fronts. There might not be a single ripple on the lake, but if Rich said, "I've got a creeping feeling," we knew to look out.

Ironically, when the wind was running high navigational decisions were uncomplicated—hole up or stay close to shore. It was just a matter of assessing whether conditions were safe for travel. That wasn't always easy, because we were still learning the limits of "safe," but at least the criteria for making a decision were known. However, good weather caused a dilemma. The Black Island incident had shown how rapidly things could deteriorate, but sometimes an irregular coastline made it difficult not to take chances. In a compromise between distance and risk, we continued to cut bays, but did so with caution, an escape plan, and a lot more fear. Granted, no escape plan was worth a crap if the wind turned and blew us out to sea, but maybe our anxiety would be enough to satisfy the witch.

Nights ended late and days began early on Lake Winnipeg; five or six hours of sleep was the norm. Because the sun barely dipped below the horizon at night, there was plenty of daylight to paddle, and little darkness for sleep. If someone got up in the morning and the prospects looked promising, he woke the rest—sometimes a formidable job, depending on how eager others were to greet the day. The time-honored tradition for rousting campmates is to throw rocks against the tent, but because our tents were cheap and easily damaged, we resorted to tossing insults instead. Hank had a different wake-up method, serenading us to arms with stirring renditions of popular, and not so popular, songs.

In the quest to push forward, lunch was reduced to a light snack, or nothing at all. Building a fire and cooking would have stolen more than an hour of precious travel time. A two-meals-per-day regimen saved time, but fell short of the nourishment required to fuel fourteen-hour paddling marathons. After one particularly grueling stint, I found Keith sitting cross-legged on a boulder, eyes glazed, the big cooking pot resting on his knee. As I picked up the dirty dishes, his eyes never moved. He kept holding the empty pot and staring forlornly into space. I wondered what restaurant he was visiting.

Now that supply points were limited, our menu had changed. We ate pancakes or oatmeal for breakfast—no more eggs and bacon. Although pancakes took longer to cook, we suffered from the "hungry-an-hour-later" syndrome with oatmeal. Preparing pancakes over an open fire was tricky; the heat had to be just right. Too hot, and the birds got a scorched treat. Too cold, and they got a doughy treat. To the dismay of many birds, our constant hunger led to lenient definitions of scorched and doughy. We topped our pancakes with homemade syrup, fashioned from water, sugar, and a few drops of concentrated maple flavoring. The runny concoction would be an affront to any self-respecting Vermont maple tree, but it really didn't taste all that bad. Or, to be accurate, it wasn't offensive. Somehow I ended up as designated pancake cooker, and the buttermilk delights became known as "Dennycakes." I'm not sure if that was a term of endearment—and I didn't ask.

For dinner, we ate anything that could be combined or supplemented with macaroni, rice, or instant mashed potatoes, all portable and cheap foodstuffs. Popcorn quickly became a favorite dessert, and a staple. Unpopped, it was compact, and took up little space in the pack; when popped, it looked like a feast. We rationed our freeze-dried food carefully. When it did grace a meal, one packet of the precious stuff was dumped into the largest pot, which was then filled with macaroni or rice. The freeze-dried food was for spice, the rest for bulk. We discovered that diluted freeze-dried food often tasted like dead pine needles, but it was preferable to the military C-rations that a friend had given us to try—the Army didn't eat any better than we did. For meals requiring flavor surgery, we piled on Lawry's Seasoned Salt, which makes anything taste like Lawry's Seasoned Salt.

Lake Winnipeg continued to enthrall us. Keith pronounced, "Her immense beauty is only equalled by our desire to conquer her." Hundreds of coastal islands, some no more than a boulder and shrub, created as many unique places. Between the teeny islands, flat shelves rose to within inches of the surface. When the water was still, we could slip over these, watching minnows scoot below. Cormorants dove for dinner in the shallows, and pelicans skimmed the surface. Neither seemed concerned with our passing.

Wildlife abounded on land as well. An eagle relaxed on a dead tree branch, scouting for a meal. Skirting the shore led us past moose, and a black bear with two cubs. The bears reminded us that we needed to store food safely at night. Although black bears were more likely to hang around a crowded park than to stumble upon a single camp in the wild, a successful food raid would be disastrous. To combat the threat, we developed a procedure for verifying that the food pack was hung out of reach. Keith held his arms up, and if he couldn't touch the pack, then it was safe from bears and—as Hank declared—me. Any creature that could reach higher than Sasquatch Keith was one that we didn't care to meet, and if it chose to chew on our food pack instead of any tasty canoeist that happened to be sleeping (or having a heart attack) nearby, that was okay.

∞

THE HESITANT SUMMER finally arrived, turning forests green and lush. One splendid day in particular reminded us just how far away home was. A cheery breeze was pushing gently from the southwest, and long, wispy clouds stretched across the sky. The day was warm enough that we traveled the cold lake in short sleeves. Suddenly, in the protected shade around Flathead Point, we spied a snowbank. Here it was, halfway through June, and drifts still lingered. Of course, we couldn't let this opportunity pass, so we stopped for a snowball fight. Chipmunks scurried for cover, then stuck their heads out to get a look at the kooks pelting each other with white rocks. For a moment, I imagined my friends back home, pulling weeds in soybean fields in the stifling, humid air, or choking on dust while stacking bales of hay in a suffocating barn. Poor suckers. I grabbed two more snowballs and charged.

Berens River, an isolated settlement about two-thirds of the way up the lake, provided a much-needed afternoon break. Located deep in a rock-infested bay, it is protected by a thin barrier peninsula called Sandy Bar and a large island several miles offshore. Its shielded waters are the last call for the faint of heart before entering the *really* big water. Berens River used to be a stop for steamships ferrying passengers and supplies up and down the coast. I could imagine its residents rushing to the dock to greet new arrivals, each ship a lifeline to the rest of the world. No roads came to the village in 1979, so much was still as it was years ago. An airstrip had cut into lake-bound travel and trade, but people and products still moved by boat.

Not far into the bay, a drab building of unknown use clung to one of the many bare-rock islands. Reaching the mainland, we stopped first at a small, dusty tan structure. Simple wooden steps climbed to a pair of austere doors. This was the Hudson's Bay Company, home to traders for three hundred years. To locals, it was probably just the village store, but to us, the name was magic. Inside, a handful of closely spaced shelves containing food, clothes, and hardware rose from the floor. Here was a little of everything, but just a little. A hearty aroma filled the room, reminding me of general stores I visited as a child. Basking in a way of life that was nearly extinct, we picked out supplies. We remained under control until we hit the cookies and candy. Spying the source of cosmic energy, we suddenly became six years old. Keith bought every Snickers bar in the place, and when we saw a cooler with ice cream sandwiches, I bought two. We were like those elephants that walk for days to eat a particular dirt that contains the minerals they crave. Our dirt was sugar.

Hauling our loot to the canoes, I felt a little guilty for decimating the sweets. What if some kid came in tomorrow, looking for a favorite treat? Then I thought of how happy his mother would be. "Look, Billy, they're all out of candy! Let's just get you some nice potatoes and rice." I congratulated myself for preventing the spoiling of a child, and ate my second ice cream.

Before leaving, we went in search of the hot meal that a store clerk had said might be found at the old hospital, which was being remodeled into a lodge. The white building stood nobly along the shore, a reminder of its importance in days past. No sign hung on the door, so we knocked and cautiously stepped inside. A pleasant woman greeted us, and we inquired about a meal. Raising an eyebrow, she offered, "Dinner will be ready in an hour. Pork chops fine?" I think I drooled.

Down a short hallway, she seated us at the single long table in the dining room. The furnishings were solid and inviting, and almost immediately, memories of another era floated from the walls. Maybe a nurse had attended to a steamer captain in this very room, or set the broken arm of a boy who had misjudged the rocks while swimming. Across the table, a man slouched in a chair. In the corner, a young woman sat quietly. We struck up a conversation with the man, who informed us that Georgia, our cook, was a teacher at the school. Her husband, Jack, was a pilot. They were opening a lodge and guide service, and he was their guide. The man was a little reserved at first, but after learning of our trek and how quickly we had reached Berens River, he warmed to us. He described the Hayes River, which would take us to Hudson Bay. It was our first conversation with someone who had actually been on the waters we planned to travel, and it felt good to have gained his acceptance. He also warned us that we might still encounter icebergs farther north on Lake Winnipeg. Icebergs? Chuckling, he added that he heard it was 100 degrees in Sioux City, Iowa, that day. A cool lake breeze filtered through the open windows, and we all grinned.

The woman in the corner had something to do with the school and was waiting two days for a plane to fly out. She only spoke when spoken to, and looked frail and ill-suited for the harsh environment. In contrast, Georgia laughed and beamed. Some people are cut out for this life. Some aren't.

Georgia's pork chops, potatoes, and peas were tasty. We gorged ourselves for the bargain price of four dollars and fifty cents each, and were embarrassed at our manners, but it was *so* good and Georgia didn't seem to mind.

After the meal, she fed her boy and sat down to talk with us for a while. Feeling full for the first time in a week, and in no rush to leave, we stretched out in an adjoining parlor and chatted.

Hesitantly, we bid Berens River farewell. Behind us, the white lodge lit up in the evening sun, glistening like a wet barn after a rainstorm. Our destination was the other side of Sandy Bar, the two-mile-long barrier peninsula. Before we rounded the tip, a towering cloud moved across the sun, creating a deep bluish middle surrounded by silver edges and radiating "angel rays." It was just as paintings had always portrayed how a conversation with the Almighty might begin, and I quickly prepared for my interview. Unfortunately, God didn't speak. In fact, the angelic cloud grew into a vengeful cloud, a cloud on a smiting mission with lightning arcing everywhere. The bolts barely missed us, but judging from the firestorm about to hit Berens River, somebody there was sinning a little.

Sandy Bar camp taught us three lessons: 1) Sand is great for sleeping, but tastes bad (the stuff gets into everything); 2) mainland mosquitoes like to party on barrier peninsulas; and 3) a sandbar isn't the best place to be when a savage thunderstorm rips through the night.

Once past Berens River, Lake Winnipeg felt even less tame. If the wind is right, waves have more than a hundred miles in which to build their fury. The lower part of the lake is a cougar, strong and quick. The upper section is a Bengal tiger, powerful and relentless. Our first day on the tiger didn't bode well. Rough water delayed our start until late morning, and we spent the afternoon brawling with large swells. We quickly ceded the day when a cold northwest wind pushed seas back up beyond a safe level. Preparing to land, we pointed the canoes toward the sand shore. Even on a soft beach, debarking would be tricky, as breakers were pounding the coast pretty hard. We planned to pick a good wave, ride it in until the bow hit land, then quickly jump out and pull the canoes up before the next wave crashed over the stern. Keith and I grounded first, leapt into the water, and raced up the beach, barely avoiding being overrun. Just above the screaming wind, we heard a frantic call from Hank.

"Rich is in!"

Swinging around toward Hank's voice, we saw Rich, chest deep in the lake, struggling to get out of the bone-chilling water while being hammered by each incoming wave. He was completely drenched. By the time we got to him, Rich had already managed to escape intact, and even mustered a laugh.

"What happened?" we asked.

"Deep water, short legs." Rich had stepped out of the canoe into a drop-off.

The laughter faded quickly when Rich began to shiver in the biting wind, which was getting stronger and colder by the minute. I was shivering, and I hadn't just taken an impromptu swim in freezing water. Our first thought was to get him into the trees, and out of the gale, but that was impossible. This part of the lake consisted of miles and miles of narrow beach backed by forest swamp; thirty feet of exposed sand was the extent of our domain. Rich would have to wait until we got a fire going and pitched a tent. Starting a fire in the gale was difficult. We fashioned a small windbreak out of the canoe covers and driftwood, providing just enough protection to coax forth flames. Once a fire was going, the windbreak had to be moved back so it wouldn't burn. With flames unshielded, the wind, now up to full howl, callously stole the fire's warmth.

Pitching a tent in such wind was equally challenging. The flimsy material went up excruciatingly slowly, insolently slapping us the whole time. Twice we had to retrieve the rain fly from the swamp. In the meantime, the icy windstorm wreaked its damage quickly, and Rich began shaking uncontrollably from the cold. Once the tent was in place, we stacked him under several sleeping bags and waited. Fifteen minutes passed. "How are you doing?" we asked.

"I'm st-t-t-till not getting w-w-warm . . ."

Ten minutes later, we hoped for better news. "Now?"

"N-n-nope."

This was getting serious. In our previous unplanned swim at Fergus Falls, Rich and I had shaken the chills fairly quickly, but our huge bonfire had replaced the heat our bodies lost. This time, Rich had to regenerate on his own. If hypothermia was setting in . . .

Another ten minutes passed. "How's it going in there?"

"I d-d-don't know."

It was time to pull out the big guns. Hank fired the first round. "Rich, if you don't get warm quick, somebody is going to have to get in those sleeping bags with you."

"I'm okay."

It took a while, but Rich recovered.

Mesmerizing breakers pounded all night. I slept well, except for the couple of times I peeked out to make sure that the surf was keeping its distance from our camp. I later learned that I wasn't the only one who made a habit of this. During the night storm at Sandy Bar, Hank had gotten up to do the same.

By morning, the weather hadn't changed. There was no chance of going anywhere, so we set about finding ways to pass the boredom. I patched some pants and cleaned the tent. Beachcombing was popular, providing peaceful solitude and opportunities to discover the many small things that normally don't gain our attention—a beetle climbing miniature sand dunes, the muted underside of a leaf, or water from a retreating surge disappearing into the sand. As a group, we played high-stakes poker for Filbert's peanuts, and spool-of-rope football. Soon we were throwing some pretty good spirals.

With plenty of nothing to do, it seemed like a good time to test our shortwave radio. If it failed, we would have to contact the air company from Norway House and arrange a predetermined pickup date for several weeks later. If the radio didn't work now, it would be too chancy to assume that it would work later on. For the test, we would radio Selkirk, located just south of Lake Winnipeg. There, an operator would patch us into the phone system. Once connected, the conversation was one-way, meaning that at any given moment, it was only possible to talk or listen, not both.

Our first task was to uncoil the hundred-foot antenna wire and stretch it out. The long beach made this part easy, although the wind had a tendency to blow the light wire everywhere. A few pieces of driftwood placed on the wire solved this problem. Removing the lid from the red steel box that housed the radio, I picked up the mouthpiece. It was like that of a CB radio, with a lever on the side that must be pushed when speaking. A "call" number had been assigned to us, and we had been told to follow our instructions to the letter. I pushed the lever. "Selkirk, Selkirk, this is XNR831 portable Norway House. Over."

Nothing but static.

"Selkirk, Selkirk, this is XNR831 portable Norway House, over."

More static.

"Selkirk, Selkirk, this is XNR831 portable Norway House. Over."

Every kid dreams of saying "over."

"Who's there?" a woman's voice crackled over the speaker.

"This is XNR831 portable Norway House. Over."

"Who?" She asked in a befuddled, or perhaps perturbed tone. It was hard to tell which.

"XNR831 portable Norway House. Over." Maybe there was something wrong with our number. Hank double-checked. It looked right. What if there was no record of us?

A long pause followed. We all stared apprehensively at the little box of electronic wizardry that held our fate in its transistorized belly. Finally, a hesitant voice sputtered back at us. "Are you the American canoeists?"

We tried not to laugh, but soon we were all giggling. In spite of all the formal radio procedures we'd been instructed to follow, we were simply the "American canoeists." Until then, I had envisioned a large office in Selkirk, full of stuffy operators in starched white shirts efficiently guiding the shortwave operations of northern Canada. I now pictured a lone operator at an old maple desk, and a piece of scrap paper with "American canoeists" scrawled in pencil tacked on a faded bulletin board. American canoeists—that had a nice sound to it. It felt good to be something other than a number. The test was a success, especially once the operator assured us that they were open forty-eight hours a day. Must be Canadian time.

Anxious to get back on the water, we rose at 4:15 the next morning. Once again, the lake was smooth. How could this placid, spellbinding beauty be the same she-devil of the day before?

∞

ICEBERGS! Just as the guide predicted, icebergs roamed the upper reaches of the lake. We first encountered a small one, about the size of a living room, on June 16, nine hundred miles into the trek. The oblong block rose four feet above the surface, gently bobbing in the light seas. None of us had ever seen such a marvel, so a closer look was in order. We approached with caution; remembering that ninety percent of the ice was below the water. Even so, when a sheet of white rose from the dark water beneath, it startled us. Unlike the cloudy ice above, the submerged portion was translucent, and strangely forbidding. Sliding carefully closer, each of us lightly touched the curiosity as if it were hot. Several of these small bergs strayed into our path, with the big ice floes hovering like battleships in the distant sea. Some of them must have stretched for a hundred yards. Part of me wanted to see them, and part of me was thankful that they stayed out there. Had the wind been driving the floes to the east that day, we might have been trapped on shore indefinitely. It would have been unsafe to snake through thousands of tons of ice that could crush us with the slightest shift.

Sightings of other boats were extremely rare, but while in the upper section of the lake we crossed paths with a commercial fishing boat, only the second boat of any kind encountered in the last hundred and fifty miles.

Fishing was still a source of income for some lake residents. Two men, probably Ojibwe or Cree, manned the small vessel. Greetings were exchanged in rough English, and a deal was made to purchase some walleyes for seven dollars Canadian. We might have been able to strike a better bargain, but hunger betrayed us. Within an hour, the fish were frying in our skillet.

I never thought it would happen again, but another fourteen hours of paddling on perfectly flat water netted a second fifty-mile day. We were pleased with the luck we were having with the weather, and kept pushing for every mile, but it came at a price. Short nights, long days, and a reduced meal schedule left us constantly exhausted. Sometimes I closed my eyes while paddling and almost drifted off to sleep. Everyone was losing weight; we were simply burning far more calories than we were taking in. If we didn't get off the lake soon, something would have to give. We couldn't keep up this pace.

Along with the physical hardship came an increased dose of mental strain. Over the course of history, more trips have probably gone awry because of psychological stress than because of physical rigors. Sore arms and ankles recover quickly, but hurt feelings from a harsh word do not. "Bush crazy" is a very real thing, as is the fact that you are more likely to be whacked on the head with a canoe paddle than a bear paw. Together for nearly six weeks, the four of us were getting along remarkably well, but signs of stress occasionally crept into the open. Petty arguments erupted now and then, and the daily chatter—an important stimulant—had decreased significantly, leaving plenty of time for the mind to wander. To satisfy the void, we sought new input of any kind. Simple things, like the name of an inlet called Whoopee Harbour, amused us for hours. For me, the long days on Lake Winnipeg were especially taxing, because, with the exception of working at the same restaurant, I didn't share a common background with the others and couldn't partake in their reminiscences of hometown escapades. Daydreaming worked for a while, but a point came when the brain took a nap. Once that shutdown occurred, paddling became trancelike, an involuntary action. Vision narrowed and blurred. Time passed painfully slowly, even in the presence of natural marvels.

Despite the perpetual aches and hunger, a camp like our last one on Lake Winnipeg made it all worthwhile. Sitting atop a stony shore illuminated by a huge setting sun and serenaded by softly lapping waves, we celebrated our second fifty-miler by opening a bag of Fig Newton cookies, saved for a special occasion.

Lake Winnipeg disappeared from sight on June 17, just ten days after we'd left the Red River delta. "Goodbye, you charming, cranky old bat!" Waving farewell, we cursed it again for nearly drowning us (now off the lake, we deemed this safe), and blessed it for being so generous. We'd spent just two days weathered in. That fact, plus the relentless paddling, was going to cost me at Norway House. Hank had won our bet.

During those arduous days, we forged mutual respect with Lake Winnipeg. We felt worthy to pass, but accorded the lake the humility demanded of its servants. Lake Winnipeg began as a stranger to us, but had become a neighbor—not always a friendly one, but a neighbor nonetheless.

CHAPTER 9

Canadian Mounties
and Rye Whiskey

"DIDN'T WE PASS that island once already?" I said, squinting in the cloudy dullness, wishing I had a pair of those X-ray glasses that were always advertised in the back of Superman comics.

"I don't think we're lost," replied Rich. "We just don't know where we are."

A rookie explorer might have laughed this off as another Richism, but we had been traveling long enough to realize the subtle distinction. One is an admission you're screwed, and not likely to be unscrewed anytime soon. The other means you still have a ten percent chance of lucking out.

The origin of this exchange was Playgreen Lake, said to have swallowed many hapless souls who became lost in its island maze. Viewed from the air, the islands are neat and orderly. From a canoe, they were dancing ghosts that vanished, then rematerialized in another form. They easily blended into the mainland, creating false bays, or disappearing from sight completely. Several islands over-lapped to produce fake coastlines, concealing essential landmarks behind. Because of these deceptions—for which islands show absolutely no remorse—island navigation required constant vigilance. If we lost track of our position for even an instant, finding it again was like trying to put together a jigsaw puzzle that is different from the picture on the puzzle box. Playgreen Lake was a gargantuan puzzle, clogged with hundreds of islands that all looked the same. We eventually found the passage, although we swore we'd paddled in a circle to get there.

On Little Playgreen Lake, near the outlet to the Nelson River, sits the village of Norway House. To the south is the entire Lake Winnipeg drainage; to the northeast is a series of rivers running to the ocean. The crossroads was a natural portal for trade moving to and from York Factory. The Cree knew this area well, but Hudson's Bay Company didn't build there until 1814. For the first century of its existence, the Bay Company was content to stay at the coast, letting trade come to it. In contrast, French traders moved inland, establishing trade and personal contacts with native tribes. French successes eventually drove Hudson's Bay Company to build permanent inland posts. Though the fur trade had faded by the time of our arrival at Norway House, many residents still engaged in traditional hunting, fishing, and trapping.

Approaching the remote village's waterfront, we spied something so odd that we thought it must be a mirage.

Parked on a short rise was an old orange school bus, topped with a sign that said "Yogi's." On the left side of the sign was a picture of Yogi Bear, of Jellystone National Park fame. Underneath, a handwritten menu advertised HAMBURGERS and HOT DOGS. Real or not, at that point, even a mirage dog looked tasty. Applying the brakes, we pulled into a stubby dock and made our way up to a decaying plywood platform that extended from the bus. Ordering at a narrow countertop that jutted from one of the windows, we chuckled at how entertained Yogi's creators would be to see his picture in such an isolated place, and on a school bus/hot dog stand. I doubted that the cartoon industry officially endorsed this collaboration, but Yogi sure made a tantalizing burger.

As we ate at a hand-fashioned picnic table, a truck pulled up on a reddish dirt road behind the bus. Out stepped a sturdy young man with short dark hair and dressed in a Royal Canadian Mounted Policeman uniform. Controlled, but cordial, he offered greetings and asked what brought us to Norway House. While Hank explained, the Mountie stretched to see the flags on our canoe bows, and nodded in approval. The law was on our side.

My traveling companions were intent on making sure I paid up on the bet for conquering Lake Winnipeg in ten days, and it wasn't long before they questioned the Mountie.

"Is there any place we can get a drink?"

Eyeing the youngsters before him deliberately, the Mountie answered. "Yes, but I don't suggest you go there. It can get pretty rough." He stared, watching for an indication that we would heed his advice. When it didn't come, I thought I heard him groan. Hey, a bet is a bet.

"What about a place to camp?" We had our priorities.

The Mountie thought for a moment. "The best place is on our land at the station—nobody should disturb you there. Just keep paddling, and you'll come to a flag on a point."

This seemed a little overprotective, but fur-trading outposts had a history as colorful as any frontier town. It was alleged that when York boat brigades converged on Norway House, the men would get their rum rations and spend all night drinking and fighting with old friends. According to one story, the men were kept from bothering anyone else, confined to an island aptly named Drunken Island. York boat brigades hadn't visited Norway House for some time, but this was still the frontier. Life could be hard, as could the inhabitants who endured. We were obliged for the Mountie's offer.

After finishing our burgers, we set off to check out the station. On the way, we passed a handful of buildings loosely scattered along the shore. A gray floatplane loitered at a dock, two fishing boats at another. Just as the Mountie had described, a flagpole stood amid three or four small houses and a garage on a point across a bay. Leading up to the station, a mild slope of grass barely eked out a living in the thin soil. Bedrock sporadically jutted through, creating a jumble of texture. The placid scene looked more like a place where children, not felons, bolted out a door. Only the emergency lights on a truck parked outside alluded to the station's true function.

The officers were very friendly, and authorized a camp in the grass, just off the water. After taking baths in a lake that finally wasn't so cold that it caused breathing to stop, we hiked to the hotel/bar on a dirt road that ringed the bay. A few of these local paths serviced the far-flung little village, which dug in wherever it could amid the marsh and streams. A "road" ran to Norway House—a long, muddy, wilderness track that hooked a hundred miles northwest, then headed back down the west side of Lake Winnipeg. It was said to be passable at times, but few residents made the difficult journey out of Norway House by land. Except for the police trucks, cars were rare. There probably wasn't much use for them—the nearest community of any size was a mining town a hundred and fifty miles away via the wilderness road.

Undaunted by Mountie warnings about the bar, we stopped there first, but a woman working inside said the place had been roughed up during a recent melee, and would reopen in a day.

"Hey, maybe we could get some Cokes from the Bay Store instead," I thought aloud. "I'll buy." This sounded like a reasonable compromise to a guy who stands five foot eight.

The others quickly denounced my lack of enthusiasm as bet-loser syndrome.

Meal options at Norway House were limited; it looked to be either Yogi's or the hotel. Since we had already checked out the bear's place, we decided to give the hotel a try. Dinner was served in a small plain room facing the water. For most patrons, the meal was entirely adequate, but the food was expensive at six dollars each and on the light side for our voracious appetites. It was exactly the kind of meal we couldn't afford on our dwindling money supply. Still hungry, we headed down the trail to Yogi's for a hot dog dessert.

On the walk home, we met a friendly man named Pete, who was stationed in Norway House as a pilot for fire control. He spent his days flying a spotter and a student to various forest fires. The spotter quizzed the student about how many firefighters were required to fight a blaze, and where they should be dropped. Pete had earned an engineering degree, but didn't seem too eager to trade his airplane for a desk anytime soon. The north grabs some people, and never lets go. It doesn't care if you were once a carpenter or a bank president, and after a while, neither do you.

Back at the RCMP station, Rich and Keith went up to the office to see if there was any way to make a phone call to Iowa. Half an hour later, they still weren't back, so Hank and I headed up to see what was taking them so long. We found them sprawled on a couch, drinking rye whiskey with some off-duty Mounties. The main house doubled as office and common area, complete with sofa, chairs, and fireplace. Keith's smirk said it all—he and Rich had been kicking back on soft cushions, sipping distilled refreshment, while Hank and I had been sitting on a rock, swatting flies.

As whiskey flowed, formality disintegrated and conversation livened. In any small community, it is hard for a law officer to mix social and professional lives, and I imagined the Mounties rarely laughed so freely around others. We stayed late, learning about RCMP life, and of expeditions to rescue the unfortunate and ill-prepared. I hoped we weren't either, especially the latter. The last thing we wanted was to become fodder for another tale of folly in the bush. As if we weren't already feeling a little intimidated by what lay ahead, we also discovered that even heavily armed Mounties got nervous when air-dropped into polar bear country. As one Mountie explained, "No man feels more alone than when that helicopter is gone and a white bear lopes over the ridge."

Capping an already spectacular night was the most inspiring display of auroras imaginable. For an hour, we lay outside watching brightly colored ribbons flicker and flare above, each of us paddling a different river of light out into the universe. Such are things that fill the whiskeyed minds of explorers.

∞

THE SECOND DAY at Norway House was loaded with errands. A trip to the Hudson's Bay Company store netted us more supplies, including a rare delicacy—apples. Sitting on a little knoll by the water, we savored every bite while being entertained by a floatplane taking off, pulling up just in time to miss the trees. Watching this, it occurred to me that I didn't like to fly, but it was probably a little late to be worrying about that.

On a recommendation from the Mounties, we stopped to talk to a local legend who had lived in the area for decades and was well versed on the Hayes River. He was reported to be somewhat cantankerous, dispensing a wealth of information, but only if he deemed you worthy of it. Like kids presented to Grandma before Sunday school, we lined up on his porch and knocked. A gruff man opened the screen door. "Yeah?"

Hank eloquently explained our quest, but the man never looked up. He just stood in the doorway and stared intently at the porch. I thought our presentation was going well, but before Hank finished, the legend interrupted. "That's what you got for your feet, huh?" He was referring to our tennis shoes. "No rubber boots? Your feet will be wet all summer."

This had the makings of a short conversation, but before we could stammer an answer, he spoke again. "You got Berard's map?"

Hank responded with a resounding "Yes!"

"I helped make it. Come in." We had passed the entrance exam.

The ten-day conquest of Lake Winnipeg impressed him and sealed our admission. He proceeded to tell us what to expect on the Hayes. A man of phrases, he repeatedly exclaimed, "The bugs'll kill ya on the Ech." *Ech* was short for the Echimamish River, which would take us to the Hayes.

Hearing this prognosis, Keith leaned close and whispered to Rich. "Then what are we going *there* for?"

Rich whispered back, "You won't make it that far. Your feet will rot off first."

The old timer's advice was greatly appreciated, although we discarded the rubber boots idea. It didn't matter; I doubted the Hudson's Bay Store had boots to fit Keith's clodhoppers. Walking away from the house, we stepped with gusto. One of the foremost Hayes River authorities had honored us with his knowledge. More importantly, not once did he tell us to turn back, and he seemed like the kind of guy who wouldn't hesitate to do so. To further spur our confidence on the way back to camp, Rich and Keith retold the great accomplishments of the Southland Lads.

Determined to have that celebratory drink, we decided to try the pub again. Doing so was in complete defiance of the Mounties, who rightly concurred that sending four barely legal foreigners to a volatile barrelhouse was not on the list of officially prescribed tourist activities. But, nobody was going to let me renege on paying up. This was no ordinary bet. It was a symbol of pride, a rite of passage; it *had* to be done.

If we had learned one thing in the previous six weeks, it was that planning for unexpected events greatly reduced the number of unexpected events. With this in mind, we approached the pub through the narrow hallway that connected it to the hotel. An open table near that exit was agreed to be the best defensive position. In the event of a ruckus, we could get out fast, and once in the hallway, only two brawlers could get at us at once, no matter how many were behind them. Planning an escape wasn't the way we normally entered a room, but after learning of the recent fracas, it seemed a prudent plan. Keith was especially on edge, because tough guys always want to see if they can whup the biggest buck in the bar. As he said, "I figure everything will come my way, eventually."

The pub was full, and everyone already knew who we were—several strangers came over to wish us luck. One old man who spoke only a handful of English words kept cautioning us, "Careful, water go down." As he spoke, he made a diving motion with his hand to mimic a waterfall. It was the best advice we'd been given so far.

Contrary to police fears, the night was quite enjoyable. Or, it was until a man I had met at dinner the day before sat down with us and began making racial slurs against the Cree. Just our luck; I had befriended the Grand Wizard of the Norway House Ku Klux Klan. As the bigot spouted louder, several Cree stared coldly from across the room. Sensing an impending fight, we replotted our escape route. Not that we cared if the man got a lickin', he deserved it. We just didn't want to get caught in the middle. Luckily, he departed before a riot erupted. For several minutes, we feared guilt by association, but soon strangers were again stopping to wish us well.

Intending to leave in the morning, we headed back to the post and thanked the Mounties. Just as we began settling in for the night, an officer came down and invited us to join him and other officers at the house to eat some fish the judge caught. Soon, we were devouring fish with members of the mobile court who were periodically flown in to try local cases. Leading this team was the judge, a solid man with a full black beard. I imagined his courts to be no-nonsense but merciful. The slim court reporter had thin white hair and a big smile. The crown attorney appeared confident and young, not much older than we were. Several Mounties joined us, as did a comely girl who helped take care of the living quarters.

Fueled by whiskey and walleye, the party extended well into the night. At some point, Mal, a friendly chap who spoke with a deep accent, donned one of the famous red-jacketed uniforms that made Dudley Do-Right a hero to my generation. Just before we returned to camp, each of us was presented with an RCMP collar pin. Fashioned out of metal in the form of the Mountie crest, the clasp normally adorns the dress reds. Once back in the tents, we turned on flashlights and stared at the gold-colored pins. For greenhorn Yanks, the gift from seasoned Mounties was a poignant gesture of acceptance.

∞

"IT DOESN'T LOOK like we're going anywhere today," shouted Hank, losing his balance as another furious gust of wind pulsed off the lake.

Crawling back into our sleeping bags for warmth, we prepared for the long day ahead. Rain and wind battered the tents, stretching seams to their limits. Drops of water dribbled on my face, but I just rolled out of the way and repositioned a cup to catch the new leak. There was nothing else to do but wait out the storm. In the early afternoon, however, a Mountie stopped by and offered us shelter in their gazebo—a screened-in building with plywood shutters that could be raised and lowered. He apologized that it wasn't much, but was he ever wrong. It had electric lights, furniture, a wood stove, and a cribbage board. What opulence!

Off-duty officers stopped to chat, and before long, an impromptu gathering was arranged at the nurse's station. Apparently, the Mounties were out of liquor and had sweet-talked the nurses into sharing theirs. By about one in the morning, the booze was gone, and everyone turned to drinking coffee and tea, a rather strange custom to us. Just when it appeared that things were winding down, one of the women opened a locked cabinet and brought out two more bottles of liquor. One Mountie jested, "Hey, you haven't been holding out on us, have you?"

The woman turned and replied matter-of-factly, "We didn't think it was going to be this much fun."

We felt honored. Up here, liquor was not easily replaced.

The nurses were a nice bunch. Norway House duty wasn't as glamorous as a Toronto emergency room, but the girls, most of them quite young, never complained. Nancy was exceptionally pretty and had several Mounties vying for her interest. She liked hanging close to Hank, probably because he was married and therefore "safe," although Hank preferred to think it was because of his ruggedly handsome good looks (we allowed him this illusion). There was a moment of concern when Nancy said she wanted to show Hank her "little yellow fuzzy," which turned out to be a fishing lure. I left at three to sleep, before the nurses fixed a hearty breakfast for their guests, and before a hastily organized daybreak fishing expedition. Judging from a picture I later saw of Rich lying prostrate on the dock, feet toward the shore, blindly casting over his head, the fish were safe.

As morning came into full swing, the Mounties amazingly went about their serious business, seemingly unaffected by any lack of sleep. We, on the other hand, slept late and moved delicately.

For three days, the RCMPs had taken us under their wings. Our ages likely had something to do with this, but age couldn't explain the friendship that had formed, nor the sadness we felt at leaving. In fact, nothing in our trip planning had prepared us for the sorrow we regularly experienced when it was time to go. After breaking camp, we searched for a way to show our appreciation. Lacking useful skills for policing, we washed trucks and mowed the lawn. The regular maintenance man sat on a chair in the garage and whittled a piece of pine, beaming the whole while.

Saying farewell once again, a weathered Canadian flag was lowered from the flagpole, neatly folded, and presented to Hank on behalf of the post. The act was meant for us as a group, but Keith couldn't hide his envy that his brother received the flag. Seeing this, Mal disappeared, and returned with a flag from his bedroom wall, which he gave to Keith.

The gifts were symbols of Norway House, a community whose residents had welcomed us like long-lost relatives. In a land of scarcity, we had been treated with generosity by those who knew the ways of wild solitude and the pleasures of good company. Mounties, the Hayes legend, well-wishers from the Norway House First Nation; all seemed to understand "the reason why." And that reason was calling us again.

CHAPTER 10

In the Wake
of Voyageurs

FOUR HUNDRED MILES of wild land separated Norway House and York Factory, interrupted only by a single isolated village at Oxford House. Little had changed along the Hayes River since bark canoes first made the trek centuries before. Contemporary canoes were built from different materials, but their wakes lapped delicately against the same undomesticated shores that had felt the passing of ancient travelers.

Our busy days at Norway House had kept us somewhat oblivious to the extent of wilderness ahead, but within the first few strokes, it came rushing back. How would our cheap gear hold up? Could we handle the rapids? Was our clothing warm enough? Any error in judgment would be far costlier than before, especially in unforgiving whitewater.

The Hayes route begins with a short stint on the Nelson River, dominating water that ends up at Hudson Bay very near the Hayes. A deceptively tame ride on the

Nelson belied the boiling torrent that it became downstream, but we still sensed a strange feeling of power, as if the riverbed itself was moving toward the Bay.

Turning up the Echimamish at the High Rock, a soft current pushed against the bow, like a moderate headwind. For the first time since leaving the Mississippi drainage on day one, the current flowed against us. The swampy narrow passage, often filled with black water, wound between low lakes separating the Nelson and Hayes watersheds. The tight channel was vastly different from the immensity of Lake Winnipeg, yet just as the great lake dwarfed us in solitude, so did the snug quarters of the Echimamish.

In one of the first lakes outside of Norway House, we came upon another traveler. A bearded man was exploring the area in a canoe rigged for sailing. Having paddled the Barge for hundreds of miles, Rich and Hank thought this looked like a great way to travel, and decided to give it a try. Paddles became masts, and the canvas canoe cover doubled as a sail. Rich and Hank's setup lacked the efficiency of our fellow traveler's, and each time the sail was raised, the wind went down. Not a good source of locomotion, it was fabulous entertainment.

A less amusing encounter required a daily sacrifice of Lad blood to the true rulers of the Northland—mosquitoes. On open water, they weren't too bad; at campsites and portages, the bloodthirsty devils were everywhere, attacking with complete disregard for the rules of warfare agreed upon in the Geneva Convention. Any open skin was fair game, regardless of its value to the owner. Even in hot sun, we donned long-sleeve shirts and head nets on the portages. It didn't take us long to learn that loose-fitting clothing made a better shield than tight attire, creating air gaps between sword and victim. Our denim jeans were generally effective, but could be penetrated wherever stretched tight against the skin. Kneeling and sitting left us most vulnerable.

We quickly became mosquito experts, noting that Northland species were bigger but slower than those cowardly little Midwest skeeters that bite fast, then fly away just in time to avoid retribution. But what they lacked in speed, they made up for in numbers. Just as the old sage at Norway House prophesied, *the bugs'll kill ya on the Ech.* It was there that the record was logged for the most mosquitoes downed with a single swat—seventeen. There could have been more, but my hand isn't that big.

Equally famous critters created other obstacles for us. Beavers had erected dams where the Echimamish runs through a flat bog. With no solid ground on which to portage, our only option was a lift-over. At some dams, this meant balancing precariously on sticks while dragging the canoes across. On one such dam, Hank was tied to a log, hanging on to Rich's belt, while Rich reached down to grab the canoe. It was grueling, and sometimes hazardous. Rich carried several gashes from a particularly bad fall.

For dams lurking just below the surface, portaging was more complicated. Unsure footing made a lift difficult, but neither was there enough clearance to paddle over the top. Sometimes water was channeled into a small outlet deep enough to pass through, but the funneling motion also dramatically increased water speed, and we were going upriver. We developed a system for these dams: The guys in one canoe paddled up to the side of the submerged dam, out of the path of the fast current coming through the outlet, and held position the best they could. The guys in the other canoe raced up the outlet until slowed to a halt by the rapid water. As the second canoe came to a stop, the first crew pushed it through. Once on the other side, the upstream fellows threw a rope to the downstream canoe, pulling it through the gap. It was slow going, but safer and drier than trying to stand on a submersed dam.

Every so often, one of the furry construction engineers would show up to defiantly flap a tail at us. The dams were remarkably strong, and we acknowledged the builder with a paddle slap. Berard's map had said to expect a "few" beaver dams on the Ech; much of an afternoon was spent debating the proper definition of the word *few*. In retrospect, we probably should have thanked the beavers for their work. Without the pools of water they created, passage through the shallow marsh might have consisted of more pulling than paddling.

Once in the beaver bog, the river dissolved into tiny canals. Most were dead ends, so the trick was to find a path through. Sometimes water grass arching underneath the surface indicated which direction the current flowed, although movement became more subtle and difficult to read as we drove deeper into the bog. We also looked for signs of beaver activity, reckoning that the animals built in the current. None of us knew if this was true, but we found psychological comfort in taking action, right or wrong. As Hank quipped, "If you don't know you're lost, are you really lost?" Philosophy runs rampant in a swamp.

Whether the result of luck or skill, we found a pass, but only after a tiring day in which Hank took one reluctant swim, and Rich two.

Near the headwaters of the Echimamish, the labyrinth unexpectedly merged into a single slough, flanked by a band of rushes that bent in soothing waves of a languid breeze. A quickly rising shoreline bracketed the inlet, accentuating the picture. The only sound was the light wind ruffling about our ears. Crisp fair-weather clouds floated in a sharp blue sky, providing a ceiling for unimaginable serenity. It was just as I had dreamed, back on that fateful day when I took the job that led me here.

∽

AT PAINTED STONE, a person can nearly jump from the Echimamish into the Hayes. The bit of land separating the two headwaters is only a few paces across. We spent an exceptional evening camping on the smooth stone, which is said to be an important landmark in Cree culture.

Intoxicated by this spiritual presence, we reflected on where we had been and where we were going. In the morning, we would finally dip our paddles into the Hayes. To honor the event, we dug into our small supply of freeze-dried food and selected our most prized meal—hamburgers. At least that's what the package claimed it to be.

The upper Hayes is spectacular, with high cliffs towering above a narrow channel. Some of the most impressive terrain is just after Painted Stone. Unfortunately, the weather afforded little time to enjoy it. A dismal rain pelted down the whole day, and lightning periodically sent us scooting for shore. But life changes quickly, and by nightfall, we were camped on a beautiful lake peninsula, watching mosquitoes get caught in spiderwebs, listening to the time-delayed "thwack" of a loon's wingbeats as it took off, and quietly writing in our journals—all while blanketed in deep crimson from an emerging sun. Inland twenty yards, the tents rested on a cushiony bed of pine needles under a stand of stately trees. It was our own national park.

After sunset, Hank fished from the sandy bay that linked our park to the mainland, and uncharacteristically, I joined him. Fishing wasn't my thing (that gene went to my younger brother Pat), but it was such a perfect night. Casting from shore, I was taken back many years to our family trips to Minnesota, where I would row out to the rice bed, drop an anchor, and cast away while the last light of day washed over tiny cottages nestled along the shore. Sometimes I didn't even fish, but just basked in the peace. For a boy, those were times when the world was his alone. Rekindling that feeling a decade later, I didn't care whether I caught anything, and was indifferent to the walleye that hit my line. Throwing it back, we kept fishing, just for fun.

A growl in my stomach brought me back to the present, and a couple of walleyes later, I leaned close to Hank. "If you clean 'em, I'll cook 'em."

Hank turned and yelled toward camp, "Walleye run! Denny's hungry!" and soon everyone was throwing out lures. Cooking by firelight, our second supper of the day was eaten under the stars. Nighttime cooking wasn't without hazards—we didn't always remember to lift mosquito head nets before eating. "Walleye run" became an instant classic, a story to be retold whenever anyone thought I looked hungry, which was quite often.

The Hayes continued through a mixture of majestic lakes and rapids, presenting, as Rich said, "A picture around every corner." Some of the early rapids were pretty tame and provided a valuable education for whitewater fledglings like us. We were tentative at first, but as we learned to read the water, navigation lines became more aggressive. Sometimes we didn't agree on which track was best. One day, Keith and I portaged around a shallow stretch of fast water, when Hank and Rich decided to slip through a narrow slit between two very large boulders. The opening was about twenty feet long, five feet vertical, and looked to be just barely three feet wide. Water churned as it raced through. Fearful that the canoe might become wedged and that water pressure would either crush the sides or trap the boat permanently, Keith and I recommended a portage.

Not convinced of our assessment, Hank shouted up to Rich, who was in the front, "Can we make it?"

Rich studied the gap for a moment. "Yup."

Amid protests, in they went. With no room to paddle, they grabbed the rock sides and slowly worked their way through. Keith and I nervously watched them wiggle along until they had just two inches of side clearance.

Keith shook his head. "I don't know, guys. That's looking pretty darn close."

"We'll make it!" proclaimed Hank. And they did, but not until after they demanded we take a picture documenting the feat. Of course, for the rest of the day, Rich and Hank were insufferable, considering themselves the undisputed river kings, entitled to royal admiration.

∞

WE HEARD THE roar of falling water up ahead, yet as the river rounded the bend, it appeared to fade harmlessly into the base of a cliff. Robinson Falls is the largest drop on the river, but the only visual indication from a canoe were huge slabs of sheared rock piled below the approaching vertical face. The inconsistency between sight and sound was odd, as if the planet had gone off-axis. Still sharp-edged, the mammoth geometric blocks looked as if they had fallen just yesterday. In geologic terms, they probably did. On a human scale such time is inconceivable, but I kept expecting a new block to crash down at any moment.

With the highest drop of the Hayes came its longest portage. On legs feeble from weeks of sitting, the mile-long trail felt like five. Though lengthy, the path was in good shape, a carryover from the tramway that was built to ferry York boats across. A few iron rails from bygone times still lay rusting on the ground, slowly turning to dust. Over those very rails traveled countless trippers before us, men whose lives made history, but whose names did not.

Now boasting a thousand miles of experience, our woodsman skills were improving. Keith and Rich could whip up a fire in minutes, and procure enough wood for the night in another fifteen. We were much better at judging paddling speed, and estimating distances across water. The latter is crucial to canoe-based explorers, but isn't instinctive. Maybe growing up on a lake would have helped, but maybe not. In an era of cars and motorboats, distances weren't as relevant.

No skill is more important than selecting a campsite—avoiding disaster is easier than fixing it. Boy Scout manuals tell you what to look for, but campsite selection is an art of compromise. Inland sites are protected from wind, but bugs love them. Rain-buffering trees are targets for lightning. Dry, high ground is often exposed, low spots can become mush in rain, and bedrock that sheds water won't hold a tent stake. Fortunately, we rarely had to make the biggest compromise—picking a camp at the last minute. This we owed entirely to our commitment to fun and lethargy.

One much-loved camp was dubbed Dragonfly Rock. Tents stood high on a huge domed boulder that hovered next to the cascading Hayes. Below the narrow chute, a quiet pool provided supper. It was also at this postcard-perfect camp that we encountered a pleasantly barbaric phenomenon for which we named the place. Toward evening, thousands of dragonflies took to the sky, snatching mosquitoes in midair, from our clothes, and even from Rich's glasses (where Rich plainly heard the crunching of skeeter). Much like ambulance chasers, we were unable to tear our eyes away from the grisly scene unfolding before us. Our enemies were no match for the high-speed acrobats, who would make any fighter pilot envious. For nearly an hour, we were able to shed mosquito head nets and even take baths without fear of attack. At first, cheering on the slaughter seemed macabre, until one of the assailants made it through the security net and drilled me on the eyelid. I hastily volunteered to carry the dragonfly banner into battle.

∞

▲ One of several small hydro dams on the Otter Tail River. During the spring melt, the waters below these dams are swift.

Day one on the Red River. ▶

Day ten on the Red River. ▶

▲ An old silo attests to the fertile Red River soil.

▲ Our new Canadian friends near Letellier, Manitoba.

▲ Red River flood, 1950. The 1979 flood exceeded this, inundating more than a thousand square miles of farmland. (Photograph by Lee-Evanson Studio. Courtesy of the Minnesota Historical Society.)

▲ High water had wedged a bale of hay twenty feet up in a tree—scary.

▲ Taking advantage of receding flood-waters to cut cross-country.

▲ Hank and Keith paddle a rare straight stretch of the Red River.

▲ Writing in journals was a daily ritual, no matter where we were. This pretty spot is on Robinson Lake in northern Manitoba.

▲ An unusually calm day on Lake Winnipeg.

▲ Weathered in on an unprotected sliver of beach on Lake Winnipeg. Swamp in back, agitated lake in front.

▲ Snowbank, June 13.
Sometimes cold is fun.

Sometimes it isn't. ▶

◀ The Bay store at Berens River
(Lake Winnipeg).

▲ Long shadows mark the end of the day at a stunning camp on the northern part of Lake Winnipeg.

▲ Remnants of ice on Lake Winnipeg. This little berg was about thirty feet long. Big fellows can be seen in the distance, about a mile out.

▲ A boat heads out of Norway House toward Lake Winnipeg.

◀ Mal and the boys. From left: Denny, Keith, Mal, Hank, and Rich.

▲ Hank's duck-eater.

▲ Rich and Hank liked shortcuts.

▲ The reason why.

▲ Rare evidence of man along the Hayes route. We believed this to be a seasonal hunting camp.

▲ Rich and Hank stuck on a submerged beaver dam, going upstream on the Echimamish.

▲ A mile from the nearest land.
Don't ask.

▲ Don't get between
Denny and food.

◀ Rich received a 9.0 on this dive.
He lost half a point for his feet
being apart, and half a point for
being crazy enough to jump.

Our compact outfit was short
on space, but efficient. ▼

▲ Peace and beauty.

▲ Painted skies near Painted Stone.

▲ The Cad and Barge at a
portage on the upper Hayes.

◀ A favorite camp
on Oxford Lake.

Just an average day
in the wilderness. ▼

▲ A thundering nine-foot drop at Trout Falls. The ground shook.

▲ Rich and Hank having fun. Things got a little less fun just downstream.

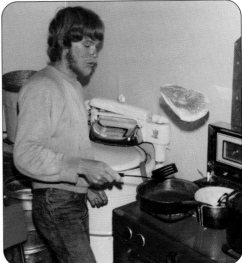

▲ Dennycakes. The caretaker at York Factory let us into his second cabin when a terrible sea storm hit.

◀ Waiting for the plane.

One of the loneliest places on earth. ▼

▲ This isn't the greatest picture of our polar bear, but Hank wasn't sticking around for a better one.

▲ York Factory today. (Courtesy of Parks Canada.)

▲ End of the trail, 1979.

ONE EVENING I was planning the next day's meal schedule and asked Hank what he wanted for breakfast.

"I could catch us some fish."

"What about lunch?"

"I'd go for a fish or two," interjected Keith.

"Dinner?"

"A walleye would do," replied Rich. Dinner was formal, requiring a specific type of fish.

Fish were plentiful on this portion of the route. On
one lake, literally every other cast resulted in a catch. As
much fun as this was, fish were a necessary part of our
diet. Our food pack only held enough to last ten or twelve
days, which was about the expected travel time between
any two supply points, given good weather and no dawd-
ling. But, Hudson Bay is noted for violent weather—we
could be stranded there for a week. Without fish, and with
no place to resupply at the Bay, we risked running out of
food while waiting for clear weather. It was important to
live off the land when possible, saving food stores for later.

It took ten pounds of fillets and two hours of frying to
make a fish dinner. We feasted on walleye and northern
pike. Canadians scoffed at pike, calling them jackfish and
considering them inedible, but we weren't as spoiled.
Hank did most of the cleaning, and Rich was the primary
chef. His recipe required pancake flour for breading, corn
oil for frying, and Lawry's Seasoned Salt for a little "bite."
Fish may have been abundant on this part of the route,
but corn oil was not, and it soon ran out. Still two days

from resupplying at Oxford House, we tried something new—boiling the fish. The Japanese ate raw seafood, and Scandinavians had fish boils, so why not give it a shot? I choked without taking a bite. Such a rancid and awful smell can't be described. I moved down by the water just to get away from it. The other three ate, rating it, "a bit fishy, and not bad." But one by one, their faces curled up in disgust, and an emergency pot of macaroni and cheese was quickly prepared. We would have to be a whole lot hungrier before trying that again!

The oil shortage didn't stop the fishing. Very early one morning, I woke up to hear Hank yelling, "Den, you gotta get out here!" Scrambling out of my sleeping bag into semi-dawn, expecting to find a moose ripping through camp, I saw Hank holding a huge pike. "Get your camera!" he shouted. "I got a *duck-eater*." I documented the event and verified the weight, and Hank released his prize.

"Damn loony fishermen," I muttered and shuffled back to bed.

∞

NINE DAYS AFTER leaving Norway House, we entered Oxford Lake, the first of two very large lakes that break up the river. At the far end of the forty-mile lake is the remote village of Oxford House, the last supply point of our journey. We could have easily traversed the lake in a day and a half, but we stopped early on the first day. The sun was hot and it was Saturday, so there was no sense rushing to Oxford House—the Hudson's Bay Store would be closed on Sunday. In no hurry, we selected an exquisite campsite on an island that ascended dramatically from the clear lake. Like mountain climbers digging in for the night, we set camp on two precipitous narrow shelves: one for the tents, one for the fire pit. Showered in sunshine, but cooled by a constant lake breeze, our split-level campsite became the undisputed favorite. A climb to the top of the island granted views that prairie boys couldn't imagine. Water and forest stretched forever, as if covering the whole world. A pair of bald eagles rode the afternoon thermals, nearly within our grasp atop the hill. Bald eagles were rare in the United States. DDT and other chemicals had nearly wiped them out. Watching the raptors in free flight was entrancing, and I fantasized about what it must look like from up there. I suppose to an eagle, it's old hat, much like city sidewalks to us terrestrials, but I wanted to trade places so badly, just to float for a minute. I think I did.

Now into July, some days got hot, though the nights remained cool for sleeping. Swimming was a perk of life on the water, and whenever we felt overheated, we jumped in. Cool water limited swim time, but that just meant we went more often to compensate. Just down the island from the split-level camp was a twenty-foot vertical cliff that beckoned future U.S. diving hopefuls—and Rich, Hank, and Keith. As the designated "keeper aliver"—a title Hank had bestowed on me after the dam and cherubs incident at Grand Forks—it was my duty to object. But the boys had decided there was diving to be done. Clear water allowed the divers to see deep into the lake, but I took my job seriously and paddled to the landing area to sound the bottom with a fishing lure to verify the depth, and to check for hidden obstacles. As I did, each diver picked his way up the slope to the takeoff platform, a three-foot square at the ledge brim. With arms held slightly off to the side for balance, the diver's eyes fixated on the surface below. He observed a quiet moment to summon courage, then his head snapped upward, signaling that is was "go time." A scream of "Geronimooooo" pierced the wilds as each leapt into the air. They reminded me of cliff divers I had seen during a Spanish class trip to Acapulco—not as graceful, or as high up, but just as cuckoo.

My leisure activities were less strenuous, and less likely to cause worried parents to visit a therapist. (Every parent has jumped off of something they don't want their kids to jump from. Obviously, we aren't good parents.) Whenever I had down time, I could often be found lounging in the shade, reading *Hear That Lonesome Whistle Blow*, a paperback I had picked up at Norway House. A history of the first transcontinental railroad, the book was thick with details, and would take a long time to digest. Density is an important criterion when there is only room to pack one book. Upon the conclusion of each reading session, the guys would ask me to recount the events that had transpired. An interesting story of greed and deceit, the book provided a daily dose of news—really old news, but something from the outside world.

Monday arrived, and our canoes ground lightly onto the little beach at Oxford House. Off to one side of a clearing was a fire tower. Beneath it was a plain building that housed the Hudson's Bay Store. On the other side were several tiny houses. Not a sound or movement came from either direction. The only sign of life was a young boy quietly fishing with a string wrapped around a can. The stillness was creepy, like one of those science fiction novels where the hero wakes up and is the last person on earth. We strode to the Bay Store, but found it locked. I glanced back at the boy to make sure he hadn't morphed into some flesh-eating creature. Uncertain what to do, we knocked on the door of a shack near the store. A half-dressed man answered, groggy and squinting in the bright morning light. By luck, he was the store manager. He explained that yesterday (Sunday) had been Dominion Day, Canada's day of independence, and, when it falls on a Sunday, it's celebrated on Monday. In short, the store wasn't open. We felt bad for bothering the guy, who obviously wanted to sleep in, but we needed supplies, and asked if we had any chance of getting them today. He took pity, and with a yawn, started to dress. To help wake up, he threw an album on a beaten old stereo. A song by Poco softly drifted out the door, and we started singing along. Hudson Bay was on the horizon, we were at one of the most isolated settlements in Manitoba, and here was one of our favorite tunes. It seemed so right.

We wanted to stock up well, because this was our last chance. If supplies ran short between here and our arrival back in Winnipeg, too bad. But, everything for sale at the store had to be flown in from long distance, and prices reflected this. Corn oil was liquid gold. To make matters worse, finances were getting low and we still needed money for the fly-out, the cost of which was a bit sketchy. Digging deeply, we agreed on a budget of a hundred and twenty dollars. That was less than ideal, but it would have to do. Seeing our predicament, the manager pointed out cheaper products, such as lard and regular flour for frying fish, instead of oil and pancake flour. Most of our purchases were staples to last the rest of the trip, but we also bought some perishables that could be eaten right away. A meal or two of real food would be a big boost to morale. Despite the realization that our grocery basket would be smaller than hoped, Hank maintained a positive outlook, as he always did.

"Whatever we don't have with us, we'll have to catch, or don't need."

That's the spirit of a true explorer, or one who has no money.

As the food was being rung up, Rich spied a cart full of "day old" candy that was being sold for a fraction of its original cost. Right on top were candied orange slices, a favorite of Keith's. A legion of other temptations lay below. Freshness (or lack of) might thwart others, but not four chaps who had recently tried to boil fish! Digging into our bankroll, another four dollars went to sweets. Justifying the purchase was easy. How else could we get so much energy in a small package, for such a good price? That would remain our official position on the subject. The manager had a different outlook. Eyeing the candy, he raised an eyebrow. "Roughing it, eh?"

Dang right! If we weren't, we'd have bought twice as much.

Rich and Keith grabbed the largest box and headed for the door, knocking over a display in the process. Obviously anxious to get back to sleep, the manager waved us on and quickly bolted the door behind us. Orange slices were soon flowing to one and all, much to the delight of the little boy who was still fishing.

Back in our canoes, a unanimous vote determined it both improper and an insult to our host country to paddle on Dominion Day. Our own celebration began at Back Lake, just four miles from Oxford House. It was possible that the scent of bread rising from the new supplies may have influenced our sense of patriotism. Out of great respect for those who made our journey possible, the Canadian flags from Norway House were raised, and we abided by the "no-work" policy, spending the day swimming and swamping canoes. Amid a round of canoe tipping, Hank laughed and shook his head. "What a circus!"

Maybe, but where else can you have so much fun?

Dominion Day marked the halfway point of the final leg, and closed with a campfire discussion of lost civilizations. It made us think of how fragile civilization can be, and how different our lives were in the woods. At home, a good day was when we dormitory dwellers whupped the TKEs in a game of pickup basketball. Now, a good day was warm feet. That night we came to appreciate both worlds; one steeped in technology, the other simplicity. Each seemed so undefined without perspective from the other.

CHAPTER 11

Fire the Guns!

STANDING UNCERTAINLY in a water-filled canoe at the bottom of the rapids, I faced upstream, frantically waving a paddle, yelling at the top of my lungs, "No! No! Portage! Find a portage!"

As the Hayes River grows, so does the whitewater. One of the worst spots is Knife Rapids, a long stretch of constant boils. We paddled the two upper sections without serious incident. In the first, we carefully waded our way down a narrow side channel. The strong water slammed us around, and the rotting remains of a smashed wooden boat created some anxiety, but everyone came through reasonably unscathed. Shooting across the current in a bold run, we passed through the second section and sought shelter in a pool along the shore. Unable to find a portage or get a clear view of what lay ahead, Keith and I left the sanctuary of the pool and paddled out to take a closer look. Intent on searching for a route, we didn't notice that we had drifted out into the current and were losing ground. By the time we did, it was too late. The Hayes had us.

Downstream, the deep blue was frosted with angry white, each riffle a potential hazard. With no chance to study the water, we headed straight down the pipe, hoping for the best. Two big rollers, one on each side, funneled into a sharp slope. The canoe accelerated and my heart stopped as we sliced into the rooster tail where the rollers met, water pouring onto my lap. Dazed, but still upright, we had a short respite. It didn't last long. Up ahead, a foaming white line stretched all the way across the river. Worse still, the water on our side of the line didn't match up with that on the other side. That could only mean one thing, a drop.

"Look out!" Keith shrieked.

"Hang on!" I hollered back.

Time slowed as the canoe shot out over the shelf and the water fell away into the turmoil below. Dangling over the edge, we realized that our best chance was to keep moving fast. Even if we capsized, at least we might carry enough momentum to punch through the perilous back-tow zone. Getting caught in an endless loop, like a log on the downstream side of a dam, would end our trip right then and there. Gravity was just about to send us crashing downward when the sickening groan of grinding metal slashed through the bedlam. The extra-deep keel of our canoe had caught the rocks. We stopped abruptly, precariously teetering on the shelf. The boat immediately began to twist broadside, which I knew from past experience couldn't be good. A second passed, maybe two, maybe an hour. Then, for no apparent reason, the shelf let go, dropping us into the froth below. The water was so stirred up that it was like trying to paddle through air. Miraculously, we climbed out of the deep hole, through the back-tow. Water again poured into the canoe as we plunged straight into a second massive wave, weighting us down until the gunwales barely cleared the surface. And then, amazingly, it was over as quickly as it began.

Having warned Rich and Hank, we drifted quietly. We didn't know if they heard us over the drone, but they weren't in sight. Shaking his head back and forth, Keith spoke first. "Boy, *that* was fun."

"Should we go again?" I uttered with similar sarcasm.

Humor was the defense we used to cover the nauseating emptiness that came on the heels of swindling disaster. Had the run been intentional, valorous chest thumping would have followed. But streaking out of control down an unknown river, heavily loaded with essentials for survival, wasn't deserving of a Tarzan yodel. Old bushmen know that caution is a lifelong friend; those who ignore it never get to be old bushmen.

Pulling up to what looked like a trail through the woods, we emptied the canoe and waited. Soon, Rich and Hank came trudging down the overgrown path. They had found the portage.

∞

EVERY FOURTH OF JULY is hot and stagnant, and 1979 was no exception. But, instead of suffering at a crowded campground, surrounded with trailers the size of houses, we were alone at Trout Falls, a thundering nine-foot waterfall. This ideal camp would become our home for three nights. A grassy flat above the falls was perfect for tents. Fishing, a requirement for any break in travel, was excellent. Lard and all-purpose flour weren't as tasty as corn oil and pancake flour, but they were better than boiling. Swimming conditions were good, although we had to be careful to stay away from the falls. There was no doubt about the outcome of going over. Some falls are nonviolent, peacefully trickling into quiet pools. This wasn't one of those. With the full force of the river behind it, a steady cataclysm blasted out over the edge and slammed into the raging caldron below. The vibrations shook the ground.

To celebrate American independence, we hung the little flags that graced our canoes from a rope stretched between two trees. No celebration is complete without fireworks; we improvised, leaving the top off of the popcorn kettle and trying to catch kernels as they erupted from the pan.

The hot afternoons at Trout Falls were filled with the usual activities, plus some new ones. Using boat cushions and metal dinner plates, we invented two games. The first was a variation of horseshoes. Cushions became the stakes and plates served as the shoes. Scoring was similar to the traditional game—a point was awarded for anything within one plate's distance of the cushion, and a ringer was any plate that rested on the cushion. A little experimenting proved that the metal plates flew better upside down. In the second game, we placed a cushion in the woods. Each player then tossed his plate, trying to hit the cushion in the fewest throws. Landing in poison ivy earned a one-throw penalty. In golf, out-of-bounds is more costly, a one-stroke forfeiture *plus* loss of distance, but we reckoned the itching was a sufficient handicap.

On the first day of our three-day stay, we were surprised to see a shallow-draft motor boat arrive at the base of the falls. Three men got out and began arranging some small logs on the ground in front of the boat. They were going to portage, using the logs as rollers to help move the boat up the hill. It looked like a lot of work for three people, and being the neighborly sort, we offered to help. None of the men spoke much English, and our overture was greeted with nervous gestures and questioning looks. Getting nowhere with the language, we all grabbed hold of the boat. At first, the men had seemed startled—a boat held the same life-giving status as a horse to a cowboy—but concern quickly turned to delight when they realized our intent. The hill was no match for seven men, and the boat was quickly delivered to the other end of the portage. With a final nod of thanks, they headed off. We wondered where they came from and where they were headed. Oxford House was only a few miles away, but how did they traverse the rapids? Did they rope and pole? Was there a secret passage?

The next day, the same motorboat returned. This time, there was nothing but grins from the pilots as their outfit was quickly lifted to the other side. Setting the load down, the men nodded thanks again, then looked at each other and snickered. Puzzled, we assumed we had done something to amuse them. Stumbling with the words, one man stammered, "Want home brew?"

Now their trips up and down the river began to make sense. The store manager at Oxford House had told us that the settlement was dry, meaning that no alcohol was permitted. These men were bootleggers! Opening a false cover on what looked to be a large live bait tank, one of the men ladled a quart of the mixture into a plastic jug. We had thought the boat seemed heavier than it should have been; this explained why. Curious as to the liquid's content, we asked, "How do you make it?"

The same man replied in the same broken English. "Raisins, warm water, yeast. Twenty-four hours." At least that is what I understood him to say, but I'm not sure enough that I would rely on those instructions to make a batch of my own. We thanked the bootleggers, and away they went. Later, we tasted the brew, cackling like a bunch of high school kids sampling our first hooch after prom. The stuff had an acquired taste, but it was the thought that counted.

Back on the move after the three-day hiatus, we entered Knee Lake, the second of the last two large lakes separating us from the Bay. L-shaped and fifty miles long, it is loaded with islands. While camping on one of them, a canoe approached carrying three men. It was only the third craft we had seen in the two weeks since we'd left Norway House. Drawing near, a man sitting in the middle called out, "Are you the American canoeists?"

"Yeah?" we answered back in voices that revealed our surprise at being so easily recognized.

"I heard you were coming through, but missed you at Oxford House."

It must have been those Mounties. They probably had the whole region on the lookout for us. For such a large area, the northern community seemed pretty tight. Neighbors might be two hundred miles away, but the gossip network still functioned as if they were next door.

The visitor was an anthropologist from Buffalo, New York, who happened to be studying the introduction of television to remote places such as Oxford House. He and his guides were on a trip to examine ancient pictographs just up the lake. The anthropologist gave us directions to find the drawings, and also told us that several archaeologists were working at York Factory. This was the most information we'd heard so far on what we'd find at the Bay. It felt good to know that somebody would actually be there. I don't know what became of the anthropologist's study, or how long he spent in the bush, but I suspect that his findings didn't bode well for the future of those unspoiled lands.

Later that day, we found the pictographs scrawled on the flat face of a stone outcrop, obviously painted from the water. Long ago, someone was at that exact spot, creating the images before our eyes. The faint pictures were spellbinding, and made us think of how fortunate early explorers were to have the help of native peoples who had made the drawings. Bark canoes were of indigenous design. Much of the food eaten by early Europeans was hunted and gathered by different tribes throughout Canada. In many ways, we owed our expedition to these same inhabitants, and said a few words of thanks.

∞

AS KEEPER OF MAPS, Hank tracked out routes and kept us abreast of how far we had traveled and what to expect for each upcoming day. Rich was the principal day-to-day navigator. We trusted both completely. That trust was put to the test on Knee Lake, when suddenly, on a rest break, Rich pointed ninety degrees to the starboard and said, "We go that way."

"Are you sure?" we asked. The furrow in his brow meant that he was still contemplating.

Rich scrutinized the map intently, then the crease in his forehead relaxed. Putting the map away, he spoke unwaveringly. "The lake makes its big bend here. I thought we were back farther, but we have to turn right now."

We knew that the lakeshore made a bend, but it was hard to see through the islands, and it didn't seem like we had gone far enough. On a lake as big as this, a wrong turn could cost hours. Plus, we had recently passed a place called Magnetite Island, a submerged geologic deposit that made compasses go every which way. Could we even trust the compass? But Rich was our man, and we made the turn. Our boy was right.

Knee Lake took a toll on us. We forgot the saw at a previous campsite, which was a serious loss, considering we had intentionally left the hatchet at Winnipeg to save weight. Downed wood was readily available, but without the saw, gathering it took a lot longer. In response, Rich and Keith devised new systems for fire building. They broke large sticks by propping one end up on a log, and cracking the middle with a heavy stone. They also resourcefully modified the fire to a continuous feed system. Large dead limbs that couldn't be broken were fed in gradually from opposite ends of the fire, elevated slightly at the fire pit. This prevented flames from migrating down the length of the limbs.

Knee Lake also took a bite out of Keith's foot, cut open by a stick in the water. Infection was a consummate worry with any injury; each wound had to be tended to quickly and thoroughly. Fortunately for us, Rich was a natural doctor—although his bedside manner usually consisted of the phrase, "Kwitchergripin'." Cleaning the large gash and dressing the wound, Rich quipped that back in the States, such skills would cost a bundle. Keith replied with an appropriate jibe about Rich's doctorin' diploma, careful not to offend the guy digging in his foot with a sewing needle and tweezers.

On Knee Lake we also noticed a shortage of one of our most essential pieces of equipment—fishing lures. Fishing lines were constantly being cut on sharp rocks, and lures got wedged in crevices on the stony bottom. This was very alarming, because dwindling food supplies dictated that we would need to eat fish nearly every day for the rest of the trip. Fish were so important to our survival that we began diving to retrieve lost lures. Once, though, we didn't have to retrieve the lure, the fish brought it back. Keith had broken his line hauling in a feisty pike, and half an hour later, landed the same fish, lure and all.

∞

ANYONE WHO HAS ever taken an extended vacation with friends or family will tell you that after two months of togetherness, there will be some squabbles. In close quarters, the mundane becomes the inane. Throw in some hunger, cold, sleep deprivation, and wet feet, and, voilà, instant argument. It doesn't matter if you've won a free camping trip with Miss USA and the *Sports Illustrated* swimsuit cover model. At some point, you will be yelling at them both. If they are sisters, they will be yelling at you, *and* at each other.

Though blessed with astonishingly compatible per-sonalities, even we weren't immune. One day, a mile from the nearest land, there was debate about where to have lunch. The conversation between the two brothers went something like this:

Hank: "Let's eat up by that point."

Keith: "Okay, but I think that's an island."

Hank, louder: "No, it's a point."

Keith, louder: "It's got to be an island."

Hank, much louder: "Dang it, Keith, that's a point."

Keith, much louder: "Hank, I know it's an island. I can see it."

Hank, throwing paddle in water: "It's a stinkin' point."

Keith, throwing paddle in water: "It's a goldarned island."

Hank, jumping out of canoe to retrieve paddle: "Aaaaaaaaaa."

Keith, jumping out of canoe to retrieve paddle: "Ieeeeeeeeee."

Rich and Denny, thankful that the canoes were still afloat, drifting helplessly away in the wind: "Uh, guys?"

Keith and Hank, now laughing: "Hey, it's cold in here."

Just like that, it was over. That's the way it had to be. Long-term memory was a recipe for failure, which is why anything said on a canoe trip is not admissible in court, sort of like when you come out of anesthesia and ask your girlfriend if you pinched the nurse's behind (thank you immunity). [On a legal note, even if you are innocent, conspiracy charges may be filed if you are entrapped into admitting that you *wanted* to pinch!] All of us barked now and then, but we always adhered to the canoeist code of "forgiveness on the water."

With the Bay looming less than two hundred miles in the distance, serious discussions ensued about the timetable for getting there. The three days at Trout Falls had been so enjoyable that Keith favored more multiple-day campsites; as the sworn Keeper Aliver, and always a bit fanatical about the food supply, I favored a tighter schedule, in case bad weather trapped us at the Bay. Plus, I had withdrawn from school, and if possible, wanted to make it back before the refiling deadline for the fall semester. Hank and Rich were undecided, but Hank, who had given up the most to go—a great job that he loved—was starting to feel like he should get back to find work. After much debate, he offered some wisdom:

"Look. We're having a great time, and nobody has gotten hurt. But, if we stay out here in the bush, something bad is bound to happen. It hasn't happened yet, so maybe we should keep going and feel real lucky to have had a fantastic trip."

With Hank's speech, we settled upon a compromise. We decided to push toward the Bay at a leisurely pace— no extended stays at campsites, but with the agreement that we would continue to relax and enjoy ourselves along the way.

Our leisurely pace lasted all of one day. Shortly after leaving Knee Lake, the Hayes became an exhausting trial of rapids upon rapids. The physical exertion was punishing, the mental fatigue dangerous. A single misread of the water could spell tragedy. To make matters worse, it was often difficult to know which rapids were navigable, and which were not. At a drop, the river frequently split into several channels, making it impossible to see past the curves and islands. Choosing a route was potluck. Pick the wrong channel, and we would be roping and wading, or hanging on for dear life, or both. Sometimes we got lucky, and sometimes we didn't.

One particularly unlucky day is now remembered as "Hank's shortcut." Just before we got to Swampy Lake, the river split into two channels for some distance, long enough that even our map showed the fork. The longer route appeared to be the main channel, but the map contained many hash marks, indicating rapids. Map-man Hank recommended the shorter course, proclaiming, "Look at everything we'll miss!" As luck would have it, our chosen channel soon narrowed into a craggy torrent that was often no more than a few feet wide, surrounded on both sides by impenetrable trees and swamp. We were constantly in and out of the water, wading in the shallows, roping from the edge, and lifting over boulders that were everywhere. Our bodies soon sported bruises from slips and falls on the uneven, slippery bottom rocks. At one of the worst spots, Rich and Hank picked their way through thigh-deep water, trying not to get knocked over by the current. After a hard lift, Rich prepared to board the canoe for the next leg, which looked deep enough to paddle. Without warning, he stepped into a hole and was quickly swept away. As the river tossed him about and whisked him around a corner and out of sight, the last words we heard were, "I'm sorry."

Not only was Rich gone, but now Hank was alone, fighting the river for possession of the canoe. Against the torrid water, the outcome was inevitable, so Hank relaxed his knees and let the river have its way. Hanging onto the stern, he lifted his legs as high as he could to protect them, and shot off downstream. Half of the Lads were gone.

It seemed like forever before Keith and I caught up to them. Now I knew how Hank and Rich must have felt back at Knife Rapids. The uncertainty of being left behind, not knowing what we'd find when we caught up, was worse than the terror of riding out the storm. For those in the thick of things, there wasn't time to think. For those left behind, thinking and worrying is all there was. Thankfully, Rich hadn't gone too far around the bend before he came to an area shallow enough to regain his footing. Hank followed the current to the same spot. With neither the worse for wear, their experience led to a new form of travel, which we nicknamed the "four loon flyaway." Instead of continually jumping in and out of the canoes, only to paddle fifty feet and walk again, we began to traverse short sections of deeper water much as Hank did, hanging onto the canoe with legs held high. It wasn't sophisticated, but it worked. That's all that mattered.

That night's camp was hollowed out of a dark, mosquito-infested swamp. A thunderstorm added the final insult to our day of torture, throwing down buckets of water and stinging hailstones. There was nothing to do but escape to the tents, miserably wet, tired, hungry, and bug-eaten. I tried to remember that the day's suffering might be the path to another day's joy, but really, our only joy for that evening was ribbing Hank about his shortcut.

CHAPTER 12

The Last Point

FOR TWO MORE DAYS, the rapids of the Hayes punished us. Islands continued to choke the drops, creating a myriad of unique pathways. Perhaps no other person had ever paddled the exact same set of channels we did, which was probably good, given that our selection was clearly *not* the preferred route.

Each rapids had its own character. Some were long and shallow, like water running over coarse sandpaper. These were mentally taxing, the riffling surface requiring attentive eyes. In times of drought, they would have been impassable minefields. For us, they were tricky, but negotiable. Other rapids were short, but hostile and arrogant, defying us to attempt a run. These were the most powerful and menacing. We challenged many, but bowed humbly to the strongest.

Our bare-bones approach to the trip might have left us wanting in many respects, but it was a boon on the portages. Our compact outfit could be quickly transported through narrow openings in the underbrush, or across a sliver of dry rock. This adaptability was handy with so many unknown channels to choose from, and rarely did we find ourselves pressured to make hasty decisions just to avoid a portage. Our style of travel reminded me of frugal students who backpack in Europe, changing itineraries on a whim. A light traveler is unshackled, and that suited us just fine.

Learning to navigate wilderness rapids is best achieved through the philosophy of Yoda, "Do, or do not, there is no try." Either you portage, or make it through. Anything in-between is disaster. For Keith and me, the lumbering Cad upped the odds toward disaster, but we were all getting more adept at reading the water and choosing better lines. At least we weren't making the same novice mistakes, such as letting the current pull the canoe through rapids. This rookie blunder could have had dreadful consequences, because to maneuver, it was necessary to paddle faster than the current. Unfortunately, this response has to be learned; it isn't natural to look ahead at foaming water and hit the accelerator. Sometimes I caught my right foot slamming uncontrollably into the bow plate, searching for the brake.

Occasionally, as we were frantically making a turn or rocketing just inches above sharp rocks, I thought of those who had made the voyage in bark canoes. The freight canoe, or *canot du nord,* was as crucial to the success of York Factory as was the beaver. Made of birch bark, and more than twenty feet long, it was paddled by six or eight men and carried several hundred pounds of cargo. How such a capable vessel could be made from seemingly fragile materials, or be paddled through such unruly water, was remarkable.

As our skills increased, so did the size of the rapids we were willing to tackle. More often than not, Hank could be heard calling on Rich to "Fire the guns!" and away they would go. At each section of whitewater, we all converged to discuss a navigation plan, then took turns in the lead. After one particularly wild ride, Hank comfortably leaned back in his seat and shook his head. "Two months ago, if someone would have told us we would go through *that,* we'd have said they were crazy." Hank was right. Whether it was Lake Winnipeg or the Hayes River rapids, things that used to scare the bejeezus out of us had become part of a normal day. Either we were getting better, or crazier. I think it was a little of both.

While deep in rapids country, we awoke one morning to a yellow fog. The normally crisp sky had turned ochre, and a roiling haze blocked out the sun. A pungent smell assailed our senses. A forest fire! We knew what it was, but where was it? The wind indicated that the fire was behind us, which was good, for it would have been difficult to retreat from a fire moving upriver. However, in the heart of whitewater, a fire from the rear was almost as bad. Rapids would slow any attempt to outrun the fire. Because Plan A (running) wasn't foolproof, Plan B was to take refuge in a wide spot in the river, holding position with anchors manufactured from rocks and rope. Hopefully, the smoke wouldn't suffocate us. After much uneasiness, it occurred to us that all of our worrying was useless. There was no decision to make; we could only press forward and wait to see what the fire chose to do. Lucky for us, the threatening smoke hung around for another day, then disappeared with a change in the wind.

∞

JULY 10: "A very wild day. Of course, we couldn't find portages, so it was push, pull, scrape, and let 'em buck. Took on major water. We think we're camped at the last falls. Much jubilation as the most dangerous part of the river is behind us."

The arduous journey through the whitewater was over, now just another memory carefully recorded in our journals. Nine weeks and thirteen hundred miles had passed, quickly at times, not so quickly at others. We set camp at Borrowick Rapids, on a flat rock sticking out from a narrow island that split the river. Celebratory singing and dancing commemorated the event, although the dance looked very similar to our "there's food in town" shuffle. A feast was prepared, using whatever was available in the nearly empty food pack. Finding a single packet of freeze-dried stew hiding at the bottom, I dumped it into a big pot of mashed potatoes. Somehow, I miscalculated how much water to add, and the final product was, shall we say, a tad thick. I was initially very perturbed about what I considered to be a poor meal on such a special occasion, but it proved to be the highlight of the night. My campmates took enormous pleasure in holding their spoons and plates upside down, shaking them, all the while the concoction clinging to the plates like fat, pasty leeches. For the record, not a single bite remained.

Everyone beamed that night, proud to have conquered the toughest portion of the Hayes. In spite of having come so far, we were immensely curious in what lay ahead. While slogging along in the rapids, our concentration had been so narrow that it was only then that we realized that if the Hayes remained fast and didn't wind about, the hundred and twenty miles to the Bay could fall in only two days. How different this would be from the slow and wandering Red River in North Dakota, where it took at least a week to cover the same distance.

Resting by the hypnotic river, I watched a little stick float by. I wondered if we would beat it to the ocean. Floundering through the turbulence, the stick bobbed downstream, free to explore another new world. Tomorrow, we would join it.

∞

DAWN BROUGHT A heavy mist to the river, turning color into black and white. It was impossible to see more than twenty feet. Tranquil but sinister, the mist quickly burned away, and with a resounding call of "To the Bay!" we loaded the canoes and nosed into the current.

Once clear of the rapids, the Hayes sprinted full-out to the ocean. The river ran so fast that we thought we could see it go downhill. How depressing it must have been to be in a York boat going upstream. Around the turn of the nineteenth century York boats had replaced the freight canoe for transporting goods inland. Made of wood, and based on an Orkney design that had its roots in the Viking longboat, they were long and shallow drafted, with pointed ends that could be easily beached and unbeached. Propelled by six or eight oarsmen with oars eighteen feet long, the boats were tracked or poled up fast water, and rolled across portages on logs, much as our bootleggers had done. Heavy and big, York boats were difficult to portage, but often traveled in fleets (brigades), so there was plenty of manpower to assist. The last brigade came to York Factory in the 1870s. Though the resourcefulness of upstream travelers was fascinating, we preferred a one-way trip.

Whether in a York boat or an aluminum canoe, all who pass the Brassey Hills on the downstream run can smell the end of their journey. Even with friendly current pushing from behind, there was an inexplicable urge to go still faster. Paddles dug deep and pulled hard. Barreling along, it was easy to see changes in the landscape. Trees became smaller and tangled. More snow lurked in the shadows. A river that had chiseled its course atop bedrock began to soften, cutting deep into clay, creating high, steep banks. Some must have been ninety feet high. Evidence of mudslides indicated that the soil wasn't always stable.

The quick pace also allowed us to creep up on wildlife. A startled goose nesting in a slide zone nearly came into the river after us. We meant her no harm, but she didn't see it that way. A graceful wolf at the water's edge cautiously eyed us, then slunk out of sight. It was my first view of a wolf in the wild; I had never seen an animal look so free.

Growing constantly, the Hayes doubles in size where it meets the Gods River. The little stream that started at Painted Stone had become a massive living thing with one agenda—finding the Bay. After an amazing seventy-mile day, camp was pitched at the Gods River junction. This was rumored to be a good place to camp, but we must have been on the wrong side of the junction, because it was pure misery. The bank was steep and rose high above the river, with no flat spots anywhere. Up top was some level ground, but also a thick swamp. Wood that we gathered without our saw was too wet to burn, and the bugs were terrible. We settled for a sloping site on the bank, then had to contend with sleeping bags sliding downhill all night. Worst of all, the sparse covering of grass was little protection from the frosty clay, and it felt like we had slept on a cooler. Permafrost couldn't have been far below.

Morning dawned equally blah—overcast and cold. How appropriate it was to freeze at the end of the expedition, just as we had in the beginning. A greatly unsatisfying breakfast of uncooked oatmeal sent us on our way into a brisk wind and spitting rain. As we pushed on through the subarctic lowlands, the trees continued to shrink and the previously sparkling clear Hayes turned brown with mud. The river kept running fast, but any excitement was muted by the foul weather. The minutes dragged on in agony.

In early afternoon, we stopped at the junction of the Pennycutaway River to set up the radio, in order to arrange the flight that would carry us out from York Factory. Doing it now would give the pilot a day to check the tide and weather outlook, and if we didn't get through, we could try again the next day. Anxiously gathered around the little red box that was our link home, Hank made the call. Pensive tension turned to relief as Selkirk answered and patched the call through. Hank explained our timetable to the aviation agent's secretary. A short silence followed.

"Call back in an hour and a half. Over."

Knitting his brow in confusion, Hank pulled the microphone close. "Whaaaaat?"

"Call back in an hour and a half. Over."

Dumbfounded, Hank rolled his head, then pushed the microphone lever. "Do you know where we're at?" It seemed incredulous to us, huddled on river gravel in the middle of the middle of nowhere, to be effectively put on hold. Hank turned to us. "Does she think we're in a motel and all we have to do is put in another quarter?"

Of course, we ended up waiting. Bargaining always favors those sitting in a comfy chair over those on gravel. Naturally, by the time we made the second radio call, atmospheric conditions had changed, and Selkirk didn't respond. We moved on, a little less certain about finding our way home.

By late afternoon, the already imposing river began to get downright gigantic. There, the Hayes decided to fight us for every last yard, sending wind and waves to greet us head on. As if that weren't enough, the Bay jumped into the fracas, bringing out its secret weapon, the tide. Hudson Bay tides could be severe, and soon our friendly current was retreating in the other direction. This was totally incomprehensible to ocean neophytes like us. Water always went downhill, and any reversal of this fact had to be voodoo magic.

Locked in a duel with the tide and wind, our heads drooped and our eyes fixated on the few feet immediately in front of the canoe. Preoccupied with the present, it took us a while to notice that on the horizon, a grey sky appeared to sit upon grey water. Fatigue and a previous false alarm gave us cause for skepticism, but slowly, everything came into focus. It had to be the Bay, and that meant that York Factory must be close, as it was built several miles into the river for protection against storms. Creeping painfully forward, we hugged the shore, trying to stay out of the wind. Being so close to the tall river-bank, it was difficult to see past any protrusion of the shoreline—hopes soared each time we rounded the tiniest of points, only to be dashed again.

Up ahead on the left, a dark figure moved. Tired eyes could not be trusted, but then the shadow moved again. It was a person! By the time we were within two hundred yards, several people stood on top of the bank, milling around, pointing in our direction. It looked like a welcome party, but then Rich noticed something peculiar.

"Uh, they have guns."

This was troubling. Were the English and French rekindling the York Factory wars? During the first thirty years of its existence, the fort had changed hands several times. The English got the last say, but maybe the French were giving it another go. I quickly calculated my own lineage. Mom had some Irish blood, Dad was German. The Irish and English didn't always get along, so that gave me French allegiance. But the French might still be a bit perturbed about that WWII thing with the Germans. It could go either way. "Are they pointing them at us?"

"I don't think so."

That was a relief, but not completely reassuring. They must have been the archaeologists that we had heard about, but why were they armed? I tried to remember where the Wrist Rocket was. If things got rough, I'd better do the shooting. Keith was only good with batteries.

Nearing the shore, we called out: "Is this York Factory?"

"Yes! Are you the American canoeists?" one of them hollered back.

"That's us."

"We've been expecting you." We laughed, knowing that our Mountie friends at Norway House were still looking out for us.

After fourteen hundred miles and more than two months, the Lads from the Southland drove their canoes into the crumbling bank. As we stepped onto the mushy ground, our weary bodies nearly buckled.

Fatigue aside, Hank was grinning his big ol' grin. "We did it, boys. We did it!"

That we had. Later, each of us would weigh its personal meaning, but on this day, there were no speeches or ticker-tape parades. Our last strokes at York Factory were taken with no more fanfare than the first at East Leaf Lake, and that was exactly how it was intended to be. I reached for my partners—a simple handshake cemented a bond that would endure forever.

CHAPTER 13

Land of
White Bears

OUR WELCOMING COMMITTEE was indeed the archaeology team. Two professors and eight students had come to search for artifacts before the sea washed them away for good. Every year, the bank eroded further inland, taking a part of York Factory history with it.

After several minutes of pleasantries, we finally mustered the courage to ask about the weaponry. "What's with the rifles?"

"Polar bears."

"Oh . . ." My mind flashed back to the huge and terrifying beast we had seen at the natural history museum in Winnipeg. "Are they around?"

"None yet, but it's about time. Once the ice breaks up in the Bay, they come to the mainland. Just up the coast from here, they're thick."

As we chatted, I got my first look at York Factory. Scrub trees and brush enclosed a flat, grassy clearing. We weren't quite in the treeless tundra yet, but it wasn't far away. The area around York Factory is part of the Hudson Plains, a cold wetland. Areas to the north are treeless; those to the south are low forests of willow, tamarack, and black spruce. On the right side of the clearing stood the Great House, an imposing white wooden building trimmed in green. This is where trade was conducted. Concealing a central courtyard, this particular building was constructed in 1832, and was the only survivor from an era when the riverside port boomed with activity. Two equally spaced rows of windows, one up, one down, stretched around the rectangular post, giving it a sense of organization and formality. Above the windows sat a shallow roof, which wavered slightly—enough to soften the regular pattern, but not enough to challenge dignity.

Facing the water, a taller section with three rows of windows housed two massive wooden doors. Capped by a steep hip roof and an observation cupola, this simple noble entrance had greeted all who strode up a boardwalk from the loading dock. From the lookout, one could have observed smaller boats ferrying cargo back and forth to sea vessels anchored at Five Fathom Hole, a deeper spot a few miles out in the Bay. Both the pier and boardwalk were gone now. Between the second and third row of windows hung a neatly lettered sign that read "Hudson's Bay Company, 1670." The company of traders first incorporated then, though nothing of permanence appeared along the Hayes until the following decade. This location was the third for York Factory, developed in 1788. Flooding had driven the outpost from two previous sites. Originally, an octagonal brick fort stood here, but in the short span of thirty-five years, its rigid construction surrendered to the heaving frozen ground.

Tucked away on the left side of the clearing was a smaller drab building with a tin roof, currently serving as the archaeologists' base. Coiled about the windows was a hefty serving of barbed wire, reminiscent of a prison. "What's the deal with the wire?" we inquired.

"Bears."

"Huh?"

"They get curious and look in the windows. If they happen to break one and get cut, they get pissed off and start ripping stuff up."

Maybe we hadn't thought this bear thing through. So far, we had learned that they were huge, could outrun and outswim us, were naturally curious, weren't afraid of anything, and might have a temper. The only good news was that they couldn't climb trees, but few trees in the area were worth scaling. Two of the archaeologists wore high-caliber rifles as if they were just another piece of clothing, yet all that would separate us campers from a thousand-pound bundle of joy was a nylon tent. I shuddered, then thought how amused my grandpa would be by all of this. Grandpa used to delight in telling stories of man-eating bears that roamed the woods, looking for little boys. I had known he was pulling my leg, but I always had that tiny bit of doubt. Seeing the uncertainty in my face, he would laugh until he cried. Grandpa would be hysterical right about now.

Trying to sound only as interested as I thought a brave, seasoned bushman should, I asked about bear safety procedures. "What do you do if you happen upon one?" When dealing with grizzlies, I had heard that the answer was complex, depending upon aggressive posture, whether the bear had been following you, and so on (assuming that you were able to get past the "Holy crap!" stage of the confrontation).

"You got a gun?" the archaeologist queried.

"No." I heard a few snickers from the rear of the group.

"Then you hope he likes one of them bigger fellers, eh?" he quipped, nodding his head toward my fellow Southlanders.

I grinned. That was my plan all along!

And so, this was York Factory in 1979—mostly history and bears, and not much else. Even the polar bears were part-timers, staying only for the short ice breakup of summer. Once the Bay froze again in the fall, they returned to the ice to hunt seals. What lay before us was all that time had spared. Wilderness had reclaimed the rest.

Before meeting the anthropologist back on Knee Lake, the only human we had expected to find at York Factory was a man by the name of Doug. "Crazy Doug," as he'd been called, was said to live on provincial land a short walk down a riverside path. Doug's cabin was nestled away in a second, smaller clearing. Outside it, a wheelbarrow and an assortment of old tools were scattered about. Another cabin stood slightly apart from the first, for housing the occasional government official visiting the area. Under a dilapidated lean-to, a stubby man pounded on something with a hammer. Protecting his receding hairline with a cap, he looked to be about fifty years old. Catching sight of us, he slipped inside his cabin without so much as a wave.

Undaunted by the cool reception, we went to visit, and within minutes, the previously reserved man couldn't stop telling the captivating story of York Factory. Crazy Doug probably got his nickname from a strange conversational quirk, one I suspect developed over many years with only bears for company. He often spoke to no one in particular, about whatever came to mind, whenever it came to mind. His wife, up from Winnipeg for a visit, shared this trait, though to a lesser degree. Both would talk at the same time, perhaps she about the weather, and he, his boat. I tried to keep both conversations going, but, defeated, resorted to a lot of nodding.

Doug had originally worked at the Hudson's Bay Store, and left after it closed. He returned later to find the deserted site deteriorating, and ended up as caretaker when the Canadian government took over in 1968. For reasons unknown to us, Doug had lost that position. When we met him, he was working in some capacity for the province, hoping to continue his yearly summer migrations to York Factory. We took a shine to Doug, despite his eccentricities, and accepted his offer to let us pitch our tents near the river.

An equally pleasant evening was spent talking with the "diggers," as we quickly named the archaeologists. It was a special moment for us when we signed the long-standing York Factory guest registry. Scratching our names on a faded tan page, we added ourselves to the legacy.

∞

AFTER A WET and chilly night spent crammed into one tent to save body heat, our first order of the new day was to radio again for the plane. This time the call went through. Pickup was scheduled for the next day, during high tide.

Successful completion of the call was a huge relief. The only other ways out of York Factory were back the way we came, or via the Nelson River. The Nelson empties into Hudson Bay just a few miles around the point from the Hayes, but getting there is treacherous. The point is the Venus flytrap of the sea, sensually inviting unsuspecting mariners inside, then swallowing them. Men have died making the hazardous paddle. Storms can blow up in minutes, but they are the least of the dangers. Severe currents and savage tides can also quickly pull a boat far out to sea or leave it helplessly stranded miles from shore on the mud flats. Should canoeists actually succeed in arriving at the Nelson, they would then have to paddle upstream a hundred miles, against powerful current and through rapids, and hike to the railroad that runs to the town of Churchill, polar bear capital of the world. A scheduled pickup from the Bay was extremely good news.

The rest of the day was free, ours to enjoy. Doug lit a blowtorch, heated one of the few remaining York Factory branding irons, and branded our paddles—the ultimate souvenir. Later, he and a quiet man named Jim took us on a tour of the Great House. I wasn't sure who Jim was, or how he fit into the picture. He stayed in the cabin with the archaeologists, although he didn't seem to be one. Maybe Jim was Doug's replacement, and the diggers were staying with him. Introspective, Jim was quite a contrast to the brash Doug. Despite their personality differences, both knew and loved York Factory.

Inside the Great House, we stood in silent awe upon the planked floor that had felt the feet of sea captains, clerks, and Cree traders. I could picture a fresh crop of York boaters, wild with anticipation and eager to prove their worth. Tribal middlemen might have bargained for a better price over by the entrance. Cargo handlers may have unloaded a cart of blankets on the very spot I stood. Piled on tables throughout the building were artifacts from previous generations—utensils, tools, and many things foreign to those who had never used them. Leave it to Rich to sniff out a hundred-and-twenty-five-year-old beer bottle. A climb up a ladder to the observation cupola provided a full-round view of the area—river and Bay in one direction, low muskeg everywhere else.

Despite its age and the harsh climate, the building endured. Built in sections designed to "float" on the unstable frozen ground, its wooden construction conformed to nature's will, unlike the original rigid brick fort, which fought nature and lost.

From a doorway leading into the center courtyard, I heard a wavering voice. "You gotta come see this." Approaching the door, I peered to see what caused the commotion. Stained into the far wall was the outline of a polar bear skin that had once been tacked up to dry. For perspective, Keith trudged across the quadrangle and stood next to the skin's outline. His meager six foot nine frame was no match for the king.

A walk to the cemetery capped our tour. There, the days gone by felt eerily close to those present, as if blurred by a time warp. Rows of grave markers that once stood in straight lines, now staggered drunkenly in the constantly shifting permafrost. The graves of children brought harsh reality to an idyllic image of voyageur life.

An archaeology lesson filled out the afternoon. Some of the diggers meticulously labored in six-foot squares, brushing away tiny layers of York Factory archive. Compared to the volume of hidden artifacts that must lie under every footstep, the tiny plots seemed so futile. A more aggressive form of archaeology was to our liking—beach combing. Why sift through all of that dirt, when the Bay will do it for you? Beach combing at low tide was a ritual for everyone at York Factory, and at Doug's invitation, we joined in, scouring the newly eroded bank. Down the coast, diggers did the same. How strange the human psyche is. Put a common table knife in the earth for two hundred years, and it becomes precious. It is a tribute to man's need for feeling connected to the past—either that, or we are just dumb.

Toting along the last of our popcorn to offer as a treat, we concluded the day with a visit to the diggers. A big hit, the corn was popping on the stove within minutes. I joined a card game of Rummy Royal taking place on the floor in the living room/kitchen. Eleven people shared the coed house, and as we played, I wondered how they would fare in the tight quarters. Friendships were developing, cliques were forming, and there was even some romance in the air. As one of the girls played coy with her favorite beau, I thought about their future. Back home, an unwritten rule in the musician's code of conduct was, "Never date a member of the band." The very things that attract people in stressful situations can reverse polarity awfully fast. Just like a band, the Bay presented ideal conditions for polar shifting. I hoped it worked for the blooming couple. If it didn't, heaven help the lovers, and those trapped in the crowded house with them.

∞

JOURNAL ENTRY for Saturday, July 14:

> "We are still here. This morning we were soaked and
> dangerously cold, as a sea storm is hitting us hard.
> Nobody slept a wink, and our tent was literally float-
> ing in a pond. Swallowing our pride, we asked Doug
> for help, and he let us into the second cabin. The
> weather has gotten worse all day. Near freezing con-
> ditions, and three inches of rain so far, driven by a
> steady thirty-knot wind and increasing. If we hadn't
> had a place to seek shelter, we would be fighting for
> survival. Don't know when we will get out."

Vicious storms stalk Hudson Bay, inundating the
coast with snow or icy rain any time of year. Snow would
have been preferable to rain. Frozen ground doesn't ab-
sorb water, and on the flat terrain, there is no escaping the
pooling precipitation. Water sits everywhere, which is
probably why at one time York Factory had an extensive
boardwalk system. Maybe the wise man back at Norway
House had a point—rubber boots would have been nice!
Not only was it impossible to find dry land, there was no
place to hide from the wind. The gale drove raindrops so
viciously that they stung our bare faces like angry wasps.
This unstable and dominating climate made us feel vulnerable and small.

Unheated, the spare cabin wasn't much warmer than
the outdoors, but it was dry, making it as good as any
Riviera resort. There were cots for sleeping and a propane

stove for cooking. Though now equipped with "instant" fire for cooking, there wasn't much left in our food pack to cook. I admit to taking a tiny bit of satisfaction in being accurate about stretching the food reserves, but that didn't make us any less hungry. What we did have was some flour, sugar, and lard. Lying on a cot, I casually recounted the days when Mom and Grandma plied us with donuts, using these, among other, ingredients. As the first scent wafted from Grandma's kitchen windows, neighbor kids would magically appear from all over. As I salivated at the memory, Hank suddenly perked up. "How did you make those donuts?" he asked.

"I don't know. I just ate."

"Let's give it a whirl. Tell me what you know!" A resourceful Hank made a heavy dough from our limited pantry, and we fried some sugar donuts. They were fantastic—not Mom-fantastic on a pleasant summer afternoon, but for a day at the North Pole, they were exquisite.

The storm dragged on all day, the boredom suddenly interrupted by a wet and frantic Doug at the door. "My boat is sinking!" he cried. Sure enough, his motorboat rocked on the shore, half filled with water, the river wrenching hard at the mooring rope. With no dock, the boat normally floated up and down with the tide, anchored by a rope attached to a large stake on shore. The stern was already completely submerged, so bailing would have been futile, as the river would simply replenish everything we removed. Once the incoming tide grabbed the sinking boat, no rope would be able to hold it. Jumping into the water, we struggled to find solid footing as waves knocked us about. We heaved, but nothing budged. The water inside must have weighed at least a ton, and the tide was already high enough that the boat rested against a steep part of the shore. To be effective, any lift had to go mostly vertical. For half an hour, we tried every combination of science and brawn. Lightning flashed and hard stones of ice pelted us from above. A few feet away, part of the soft bank caved in. Once in a while, above the din, Hank could be heard whistling Billy Joel's song, "The Stranger." Hank didn't know why he whistled, but the haunting melody made the moment even more bizarre. Drained and numb, we gave one more Herculean effort, and the boat finally slid above water. A grateful Doug jumped about in joy.

By the next morning, the storm had passed. I read my book by the river while drying everything out, then decided to walk down to check on the diggers. They were pretty dejected. The storm had completely washed away a dig by the water. A mosquito tent lay crumpled and torn in a wet pile, ripped away by the wind. As we spoke, a loud clap pierced through the silent aftermath, coming from the direction of Doug's place. Then another, and another. Gunshots? All sorts of tragic scenarios crossed my mind. Had Doug gone mad? Had pirates sailed upriver? Not being able to take the suspense, I started back down the trail toward Doug's, jumping nervously at every cracking twig, and muttering to myself that I was as stupid as those people in horror movies who just have to go check out the monster in the basement. Halfway, I was met by Doug, Hank, Keith, and Rich, all as excitable as my hypoglycemic roommate when he ate a whole bag of Oreos. "There you are!" they cried. "We thought you got eaten by a polar bear."

Trembling with excitement, they retold the story. They had been in the cabin, when Doug swung the door open and yelled, "Here's your bear, boys!" Scrambling out, they got a good look at a massive white bear heading toward the river. Doug raised his shotgun and began firing light loads of buckshot at the bear to scare it off. Each time he fired, the bear reared its head back and roared. At the river, the bear stopped and looked to the side, then slid over the bank and into the water. Doug switched from his shotgun to his rifle and continued firing, driving the bear farther away.

Disappointment gripped me as the tale unfolded. It was a once-in-a-lifetime opportunity, and I missed it. Then, it occurred to me that the bear had stopped at the river only fifteen feet from where I had been reading. My stomach knotted; I had to sit down.

CHAPTER 14

And So
It Came to Pass

THERE HAD BEEN no contact with the air agent for three days, and pickup was two days overdue. Unsure if anybody was coming, we spent the morning of day five at York Factory preparing to fly out, just in case. With our gear stowed neatly by the river, we leaned against the packs and waited. Doug occasionally stopped to visit, rifle strapped to his back, an eye out for bears. The hours passed. The tide was right. If Gilbert (our pilot) didn't arrive soon, he wasn't coming. Resting my head on a pack, I stared at the clouds high above, hoping that the agent in Winnipeg had relayed an alternate plan to Gilbert.

From somewhere in the sky upriver, a faint drone rose, and we jumped to our feet in anticipation. A minute later, a slate-colored single-engine Otter passed over, circled around, and throttled down for a landing in the choppy water. Stepping onto the pontoons, we left footprints in the mud along the shore. I paused to look at them, knowing that the tide would soon wash them to sea, as it always has.

Everyone came to see us off, and watched from the top of the riverbank as the plane taxied out, our two canoes strapped below. Turning into the wind, Gilbert pushed the throttle all the way forward, and the engine screamed to life. As the heavily loaded plane lumbered against the water, I tried to forget the terror of my last flying experience.

With only two plane rides to my credit, this flight accounted for half of my total flight time. For my first flight, my cousin and I paid ten dollars each for a short loop on a tourist floatplane to celebrate our high school graduation. She laughed and chatted with the pilot, while my hands clenched so tightly that I squeezed hydrogen out of the air. A little flirt, my cousin asked the pilot if he had ever flown stunts. Apparently, the pilot misunderstood her question, and took it as a request. Or he wished to impress my pretty relative. Before I knew what was happening, the nose of the plane pulled up sharply until the plane almost stalled. Our insane pilot then pushed into a steep dive, and rolled into a spiral. My cousin whooped with glee, while I moved on to extracting nitrogen. Cocky, the pilot winked at my (formerly favorite) cousin, "I'm not supposed to do that, you know." *No shit,* I thought. I hoped Gilbert didn't feel a similar need to impress us.

The Otter shook violently from the jarring waves, then abruptly fell calm as the river begrudgingly let us go. Gilbert picked up altitude, then swung around for a final pass over York Factory, dipping a wing to give us a perfect view of the grounds. The assembly below us waved, alone in the vast frontier. The Great House was beautiful—proud, like an old man whose prime of life is past, but whose deeds have won him the respect of the next generation.

Gilbert would fly us to Gods Lake, a remote village that served as his base of operation. There, we would hitch a ride on a biweekly supply plane back to Winnipeg. Traveling the skies was very different from being on the surface of the water. From up high, the world seemed small and impersonal, as if viewed from behind a glass door. On the ground, the world was large and lonely, but a part of our being. We could touch it, feel its emotions. A thousand feet up, it was finally possible to see what lay beyond the Hayes. Like a child's finger painting, multiple shades of green smeared the region close to the Bay. Farther inland, lakes took shape. Passing over one of the rapids we had traversed the week before, a voice piped up from the back. "I *knew* we should have taken the left channel!" What was so confusing on the water looked so clear from the sky.

On the approach to Gods Lake, the water turned deep blue, surrounded by an irregular coastline of peninsulas and bays. Flying past a small group of buildings, Gilbert turned and pulled back the throttle and we coasted down. Compared to takeoff, the landing was amazingly quiet and effortless.

Bad news awaited us on the ground: the supply plane left for Winnipeg an hour earlier. The next one wouldn't be returning for three days, and flying was the only way in or out. Asking around, we discovered there wasn't a good place to camp at the settlement, but there was a lodge with cabins for rent. Our funds were desperately short, but we decided to splurge for a night. The cabins looked so inviting, and a hot breakfast was included in the thirty-five dollar rental. We would find a place to camp the next day.

After breakfast the next morning, I lingered in the dining room, and overheard a troubling conversation. I ran back to the others, too distraught to speak. "Uh, this uh, this cabin is nice, right?" I stammered.

"It's sweet." General agreement on that point.

"And that breakfast was good, no?"

"Never been so full." "Delicious." "Only thing better for breakfast is walleye."

"I think this is costing us thirty-five dollars *per person*."

There was a long pause. "You know, it sounded like an awfully good deal."

Everyone pulled out what was left of his money and started counting. As I tallied my emergency stash, I wondered whether the lodge would make me wash dishes or clean boats. At minimum wage, two days of labor might cover my share. Then again, that's about how long we had until the next plane! Thankfully, we had enough to pay the bill, but there would be no more living "high on the hog," as farmers like to say.

Staying another night at the lodge would have turned us into lifelong sharecroppers, always owing the company store more than our labor was worth, so we prepared to find an island to pass the wait. Just as we were about to head out, we ran into Gilbert. Hearing our story, he thought for a bit, then made us an offer. "I need gasoline. If you'll cover half of the extra cost to fly it in early on a special run, I can get a plane up here late today."

"How much?" We were of course interested!

"It would be a hundred bucks, in addition to your regular fares."

It was a reasonable offer, but after the cabin rental fiasco, we were flat broke. We had only enough money to pay for passenger fares, and hopefully, for the canoes. Still, the offer was far too tempting to blanketly decline.

"If we don't have enough money right now, can we pay our half when we get to Winnipeg?" Hank and Keith's dad, Herb, would be meeting us there, and could float us a loan.

"I don't see why not." Gilbert smiled.

From Gilbert's wireless, Hank called Herb back in Minnesota, and told him to start heading for Winnipeg.

∞

LATER THAT DAY, a battered old twin-engine DC-3 touched down on the dirt runway. I don't know when they stopped building DC-3s, but Gilbert assured us that they were extremely reliable short-runway planes, and workhorses of the North. Unloading the fuel gave me the willies, especially because we offered to help. Expecting a fancy machine for plucking the volatile barrels out of the fuselage, I was surprised when old tires were positioned underneath the door, and the drums were simply pushed out. Hitting the tires with a thud, the canisters of fuel reminded me of depth charges that were launched from destroyers to blow up submarines. I kept waiting for one of the cans to rupture and send us on a charred flight across the lake.

The cargo plane had no seats, so we sat in the canoes. The irony of returning in our canoes amused us greatly. Hank wrote in his journal, while Rich and Keith stuck their fingers into the atmosphere through a hole in the roof, and surveyed the duct tape patches that appeared to be holding the plane together. For most of the flight, we kept to ourselves, each lost in his own thoughts. I didn't think about the importance of what we had done. There would be years for that. I just stared out the window and basked in the final moments, knowing I might never see this place again.

Herb met us at the Winnipeg airport in his station wagon. Determined to make good on our earlier promise to return to Garbonzo's, a pizza place that we had enjoyed on the way up, everyone squeezed into the jam-packed car and readied for the short drive. Before turning the ignition, Herb got quiet and reached into his pocket. Pulling out four envelopes, he carefully handed one to each of us. Inside was fifty dollars. In the voice of a father who was about to get serious with his boys, he spoke. "I bet myself two hundred dollars that you wouldn't make it." The tone of his words said that he was proud to have lost.

At Garbonzo's, the manager remembered us and treated us like dignitaries, albeit paying ones. He visited table after table, announcing our success to everyone who would listen. We ate and ate, savoring both the hot pizza and our tiny moment of fame.

On the way home, Herb dropped me off at Fargo, where I had left my car with my brother. Two days later, I was back in La Porte City, Iowa. Shortly after arriving at my folks' little farm, Dad and I stood outside the house, talking about the trip. Mom leaned out the open window, quietly listening. I pointed to a large dent in the canoe, which was still strapped to the car. "I'll fix that," I assured them. It was the least I could do, as "my" canoe was really theirs—I had just borrowed it.

Dad nodded, then looked up at Mom, who smiled knowingly back at him. "I guess you may as well consider it yours now."

They knew what that piece of aluminum meant to me. They knew.

It was a nice summer evening, not as warm as it could be in late July. Just as I had done a thousand times before, I climbed the sagging old hog house, and took up my perch on the decaying roof. This was a place where many dreams were born, and today, it was a place to reflect on them. Looking out across fields of green that were beginning to glisten in the hazy sunset of summer, I recalled the final words that Hank penned into his journal.

"It is the story of a journey, a dream, and of a summer. It was better than what we imagined it could be. I guess we planned it well, had good weather, and had the right personalities to keep getting along okay. The trip was not a holy crusade or a fanatical journey. Neither was it to be a test of endurance or willpower. We didn't have the help of any companies or newspapers. We didn't go to try to find ourselves, to lose ourselves, or to prove any real great point. We did this trip just to see if we could, and to see if we could have fun. We could, and we did."

Like boys in their first canoes, with nothing but water ahead, we just wanted to see what was out there. Explorers of the purest intent, we went for the heck of it.

Locked away in each of us is an adventure. For two months and eleven days, we lived ours, and did it for the reasons of boys, not men—for children possess the secret to true adventure; they don't do things for the same reasons as grown-ups. They aren't blinded by practicality, reward, or whatever else stifles the adventuresome spirit of adults. They imagine adventure simply for adventure's sake. This is what kids dream of.

Soaking in the evening glow from my roost, I realized that there would be other journeys, but none would be quite the same. Never again would there be the innocence, the fire, or unfettered eyes of youth. But as the last rays fell, there was no sorrow, for an adventure lives forever in the heart. We need only seek it.

Strangers No More

EVERY JOURNEY is a venture into the strange—new lands, people, and revelations. Sometimes strange is far away, sometimes it is hidden in the backyard, waiting to be uncovered. At each new encounter, we chip off pieces of the unknown and take them home. These tiny nuggets become our guidestones to the world, lenses into everything that surrounds us. Each person can only carry so much weight, so how many guidestones we acquire depends on how many we leave behind.

This Water Goes North is what we brought home, but it is only half of the story. All along the trail, we exchanged something in return. I had always wondered what our trip looked like from the other side of the paddle, and one night my wife posed a question: "Why not track down some of the people you met and ask them?"

After twenty-eight years, I didn't know how successful this would be. Many of our contacts were nameless, existing only in a scattering of neurons that hold their blurring faces. Even more, did we really *want* to know? What if they didn't remember us? What if they thought we were idiots? Events explained in this book indicate that we didn't always follow conventional wisdom, or any widely held dogma of reason.

From a handful of names scribbled on loose scraps of yellowing paper stuck in the back flap of my trip journal, I began searching for people I hadn't spoken to in nearly three decades. Initially, the news was sad. Some folks had passed away, such as Nick Tuttle, Gene Sondreal, Orville Nemmers, Herb Kohler, York Factory Doug, and the sage of Norway House. For others, the path back to 1979 had grown over. Maiden names had changed, or residents had moved away without a trace.

Then I caught some breaks and the list slowly grew. As it did, one thing became clear—time may have shortened the list, but it hadn't changed the character of those on it. I was greeted with the same kindness and generosity we received in 1979. Here I was, calling people we met for several hours nearly thirty years ago, asking for a favor, and they said *yes* without hesitation. Such is the magic of an adventure.

For those who have so thoughtfully contributed to this book, the Lads from the Southland thank you, again. For the nameless, missing, or deceased, you are still here. None of you will ever be gone to us, nor to the kid who I hope will pick up this book in fifty years and meet you for the first time.

I used to think that for a brief moment in 1979, the distance between Iowa and Hudson Bay was shortened. Now I realize that once you get hold of a guidestone, it is yours forever.

∞

Anne Kohler
(*Saint Annie*)

YOUR ASKING ME to write a few thoughts/memories as an addition to the book caught me off guard at first. It's the first time someone has really asked me about my very small part in your great adventure, and I hope I do it justice.

While I don't remember exactly the first time I heard about the Hudson Bay Trip (HBT), it began to dawn on me in the first two years of married life that it was more than a vague dream to my husband. This man I married had introduced me to a whole world of outdoor adventures . . . fishing, canoeing, camping . . . and while I enjoyed learning about them, I was also learning about my husband. He didn't just love fishing, he *lived* for fishing, and the whole outdoors thing.

I was learning enough as a newlywed to realize that this man I married was truly crazy enough to *want* to undertake this whole trip. However, I also knew he would never shirk his duty as a new husband, breadwinner, etc., to take this trip unless he had my complete support. I remember telling him early in the third year of our married life that if he was going to leave his job and his wife for the Adventure of a Lifetime, he ought to do it while we were young, debt free, childless, and I was gainfully employed to pay the bills. I think at that moment the HBT was actually born.

The planning took months, and amazed me with the details. I remember the volumes of maps that Hank pored over, thinking to myself they would be impossible to follow. As the trip came closer to reality, a logistics problem raised its ugly head. Rich would not be able to leave with the others at the start due to farm/family commitments. I'm not sure exactly how it happened, but as the only married member of the group, Hank volunteered me to take Rich's place the first three days of the trip until Rich could meet us in Fergus Falls.

I looked forward to a few days off and being part of the adventure. I changed my mind about three hours into the trip, after the first portage over cornfields and trails in very cold May weather. I knew for sure just how crazy they were (and I by association) when we were canoeing Otter Tail Lake in freezing cold, wind, rain, snow, waves . . . with no end in sight, the light fading, wet . . . did I mention freezing? . . . still far from where we were planning to camp, knowing we'd be setting up camp in the freezing wet darkness. About the time I was sure I would die frozen in the front of the canoe, Keith spotted a light in a cabin he knew was owned by a man from their hometown of Remsen, Iowa. Orville Nemmers was up from Remsen early in the season to open their cabin and plant a garden. He welcomed us into his warm cabin with a shot of whiskey, baloney sandwiches, and warm bunk beds to sleep in. He made pancakes in the morning to send us off, and the weather, though cold, cooperated by remaining dry on my last two days. I think I was a little scared saying goodbye to

Hank in Fergus Falls. I was glad to turn the canoe paddle over to Rich, but was a little more realistic about the hard work and danger involved with this adventure.

Twenty years later, I had the chance to once again see Orville Nemmers. He was a resident in a nursing home in Remsen, suffering the effects of a stroke and dementia. I sat down next to him and said, "Mr. Nemmers, you once saved my life." I talked to him and told him the story of that long ago rescue, and while I'm not sure if he understood or even heard me, he smiled.

I've heard Hank tell the stories of his trip many times over the years, and I never fail to be proud of them all for their accomplishment. While I recognize the absence of that adventurous spirit in myself, I'm glad Hank has it, and has been able to pass on that love of the outdoors to our children. We are all better for it.

Thank you, Denny, for putting the memories into words. I hope it was a labor of love . . . I know the trip was.

—Anne

Alan Weidemann
(Alan and Joy, Moorhead, Minnesota)

PERHAPS AS AN older brother, my smacking Dennis all over as a child did something to his brain that would cause him and his colleagues to embark on such a journey as described in this book. Or rather, was it because we had the great fortune of having parents who spent time in the outdoors; if not for their own sake, at least for ours? As youth we would either spend vacations in primitive camping sites (next to cabins) on Leech Lake, Minnesota, or in tents along the shore of the Mississippi River in northeast Iowa. Our first exposure to canoeing was in a fiberglass kayak-like canoe that our father built for us. It was easy to paddle, but easy to flip as well. In my early teens, our father took us to the Boundary Waters Canoe Area for our first "father-son" canoe trip. This gave us a chance to talk to him, as well as each other, since we were stuck in the same canoe for several days, like it or not. It is during this time that I believe Dennis started to get hooked on the outdoors and the love of the peacefulness that canoeing provided. However, I never would have anticipated what it would lead to.

When my wife and I heard that Dennis and his companions planned a canoeing trip, we were not surprised—until we heard of the distance and their route. Why anyone would canoe the sugar beet and potato flat lands of the Red River, to boreal forests in Canada, to the muskeg lowlands near Hudson Bay, was beyond my comprehension. The plan definitely sounded like disaster waiting to happen. I figured they would run across every biting insect in North America. But this was my younger brother, who I thought was a little off the wall anyway, so I just chuckled. When someone tells you he is going to go canoeing for several months, what response does one give? I must confess, however, that even though I didn't let myself admit it, I was a little jealous of my brother's will, drive, and time he had to accomplish what I knew wasn't going to be easy.

Even though the Red River valley is flat for miles, and miles, and miles, the young men were still excited when they stopped by to see my wife and me as they passed through the

Fargo/Moorhead area. You could already tell that some boredom was starting to creep in as they traveled through the constant fields of sugar beets, but this was an adventure for these young men. The freedom to explore what is "around the next bend" is what all of us would like to do once in our lives.

After they left the apartment I must say I really didn't believe they would even make it to Canada, but they did that and more. It shows that big brothers can be wrong (but not often). When I hear about the things they saw and experienced, it makes me wish I was there.

The long-distance canoe trip required teamwork, but also left each of the young men plenty of time to think, and I'm sure it affected them all differently. From the canoe trip with our father, and Dennis' "great escape" with his friends, there was one strong impact: it produced a naturalist and someone to whom the quiet sounds of the outdoors are as they should be. Dennis loved the experience so much that he bought his own canoe to get away from the fast-paced life and visit the solitude when he needs to. In 2005, Dennis and my father took me and two of my sons along the same Boundary Waters route that started it all three decades earlier. Think of three generations of Weidemanns together, the older remembering what it was like before and comparing it to the new trip, and my boys getting their first taste of it. I know from my sons that they will never forget their uncle and grandfather on that trip. It was as exciting for them as it was for Dennis and me years before. Dennis prepared the trip, complete with memories that my boys talk about all of the time.

Dennis grew up experiencing nature and life. The long northern adventure from Minnesota to York Factory on

Hudson Bay is going to be something he will never forget. Those of us who read the book will find out for ourselves how exciting it really was. In the end I think most of us will be like J.R.R. Tolkien's character Bilbo Baggins, and be ready to say, "I'm quite ready for another adventure."

Bill Thompson
(Bill and Pam, Wild Rice, North Dakota)

THERE WERE MANY thoughts that went through my mind back at that time. Among them: Why? These guys must be a little nuts.

Are they aware that there are virtually no established campsites along the Red River? Mosquitos, mosquitos, mosquitos! Dirty water, muddy shores, hundreds of miles of more or less the same landscape. The farmer's daughter often isn't the beauty one is looking for. The list goes on and on.

But I have thought about you guys occasionally (especially during the rest of that summer) and wondered whether or not you made it. What was the journey like for however far you made it? Did the friendship between all of you survive the trip? Did the evening you camped in our backyard and the trip to the Wild Rice Bar and Grill leave any memories for you?

Well perhaps your book will fill in many of those questions for me. But obviously you made it, and are to be commended for doing something that less than 1 percent of the world ever has or ever will. And that perhaps makes you more unique than crazy!

Peace,

Bill

Carole Houle Sabourin
(*Letellier, Manitoba*)

1979 WAS A YEAR of many experiences, challenges, and changes for me. That year found all area dwellers surviving a winter like no other. If one wanted, there would have been enough snow to build an impassable fortress lining the Canadian/U.S. border from the Pacific all the way to the Atlantic. You can imagine what our spring looked like once the melt started. One immense lake covered fields, roads, yards, and tragically, found its way into homes. The flood of 1979 is indelibly marked into our minds. The Red River was no one's friend that spring.

I was finishing up my final year of high school in '79. The spring flood had forced closure of most area schools for several weeks, meaning our school year was extended to the bitter end of June. My weekend schedule was one of studying, especially for biology—loved the course but was taught by a teacher with very high expectations. It quickly became clear that it would be a difficult weekend to find study time. A group of four men showed up at our milk house Friday evening, covered in Red River gumbo. They were looking for a place to wash up and pitch a tent for the evening. Much discussion went on between my family and the foursome, but especially with my brother Diny, who was then twenty years old. Everyone seemed to hit it off, so as was customary in our area, a party was had that evening . . . as well as the next evening.

Apparently, some of the foursome were no strangers as to how to have a good time. One in particular stands out in my mind, as this individual seemed bent on helping me study for my final exam! I will call him Keith for the sake of this story.

This Keith came forth with pocketsful of knowledge and expertise in the field of bio (did I say how big his pockets were?). He would ask me a question, I would give him the answer, and then you'd think we would have moved on to the next question. But this was not Keith's plan, as he had to give me his version of what the answer potentially could be! One can only imagine some of his translations of what a blood corpuscle can do, especially when it has an alcohol content of well over .08!

When exam time rolled around, you can be sure that many a chuckle was had when I was faced with the decision of either writing my answers or the ones that Keith had so eloquently explained to me! In the end, I passed the exam with flying colors. One then must conclude that studying/success can be achieved in many ways, even when not mainstream, as is with life!

Meeting this foursome was a great experience for me in many ways. It got me to think about the adventures the world has to offer right at your own doorstep. One such adventure was when my girlfriend and I packed up our canoe one day and joined a nationally sanctioned canoe race on the Red River, which started in the U.S. and ended in Winnipeg. We only joined up at the U.S./Canadian border in Emerson; however, there are many stories to be told about the two greenhorn women joining up with the professional canoe racers. What a blast!

Many years have gone by and now I find my kids also tackling some of their own adventures. Ross, my twenty-year-old son, found his way to South America last winter for three months. My twenty-two-year-old daughter is now in

Australia, backpacking for three months, looking for that country's treasures! The irony here is that in my tender young adult years, an adventure was to be had at my doorstep, literally only footsteps away. In this day and age, nothing has changed. The kids are still finding adventures at their own doorsteps. The difference is that their doorsteps were, to us, unachievable because of distance and culture differences. How the world has shrunk!

Diny Houle
(Letellier, Manitoba)

WHEN HANK, KEITH, Rich, and Dennis showed up on our riverbank in 1979, they sent Dennis to the yard because he was the smallest and least scary-looking of the bunch. They were very dirty and scruffy-looking. When Dennis explained to me who they were, where they were from, and where they were going, I was very interested in what they were doing. Dennis had come to see me in the dairy barn, while I was milking cows. So I told them I'd meet them later, outside. After introductions, I decided that it would be fun to take these guys to a social and get together with my friends.

Their overnight stay stretched into two days. We went from a social to size twelve shoes to full contact basketball on a tennis court in Letellier. (*Author's note:* "Size twelve shoes" refers to wearing empty beer boxes on the feet. Whatever assumptions readers might make about this practice are most likely correct.) Apparently our basketball skills were not up to par and not only because of our short stature. Friendships were made and have continued to grow stronger over the years. Trips have been made from Manitoba to Iowa and from Iowa to Manitoba, and will continue.

Having lived here all my life, as have the three generations before me, we have seen several people come up the riverbank. I personally can think of six different bunches making long treks by canoe. They range from the Starkels and the Iowans, who went on true adventures for their own personal satisfaction, to mercenaries who did it for the wrong reasons. The latest bunch that we met had sponsors, GPS, computers, satellite phones, and TV cameras following them. How could they miss?

I was twenty years old when the Iowans showed up, basically the same age as they were. I had always dreamed of taking a similar canoe trip but never had the ***** to do it. Their arrival was well-timed because we were at the tail end of the biggest flood in recent history. The fact that we were mainly farmers and that our land was under water meant we had time to spend with the canoeists, and we were more than happy to share a few beers with them.

—Diny

Margaret Sondreal
(Gene and Margaret, North Dakota)

I WAS BORN July 20, 1927, and raised in Polk County, Minnesota. The daughter of parents who were farmers, I attended a country grade school through the eighth grade, then graduated from Climax high school in 1944. I remained with my parents to help care for my ailing mother and during this time I met my future husband, Gene Sondreal, who was also a farmer from across the Red River in North Dakota. We married in 1946 and lived on his parents' farm, which is located on the banks of the Red River. We stayed on the farm for thirty-seven years, raising small grains, beans, potatoes, and sugar beets, then moved to town for twenty years, where Gene passed away. I now live in East Grand Forks.

One summer evening at the farm, four young fellows who were canoeing down the Red River stopped and asked for permission to camp overnight, as they were on a canoe trip to the Hudson Bay. We agreed to this and Gene offered them the shower and bathroom facilities in the machine shop. I had made a large casserole for the evening meal and asked them to come in and eat with us, but they declined. I'm sure they thought they would be imposing on us, so I had Gene take the food out to them so they could have something warm to eat.

That evening, after they had showered and eaten, they came to the house to return the washed casserole dish and to express their thanks. We invited them in to visit with us, and what an enjoyable evening it was for Gene and I, listening to them relate their experiences canoeing the river this far. We told them we thought this would really make for good reading and that they should write a book about it. We didn't like to have the evening end as it was so interesting to talk to them. What a joy to meet four young men who were so courteous and appreciative of everything.

I was so thrilled and happy when Dennis contacted me twenty-eight years later to inform me he had written this book. I had often thought about these fellows, wondering where they were, what they were doing, and how their lives may have changed.

Wayne Grzadzieleski
(Drayton, North Dakota)

IT WAS GOOD to talk to you about you and your friends' adventure on the Red River of the North. What was good was the fact that you all survived. As a person who has lived along the Red River all of my life, seeing people venturing out in flood waters, that time of year, in canoes, is a bit over the edge. My first thought was these folks are a bit crazy, don't understand how bad things can get out there, and that the river would accept them as a sacrifice to the flood god.

Malcolm Hollett
(Mal, Norway House, Manitoba)

THE LOCAL Royal Canadian Mounted Police detachment and housing for married officers is situated on a point of land directly between the Rossville Native Reserve and the Jack River Métis settlement, all of which compromise Norway House. The area has a history dating back to the times when fur traders traveled from southern Manitoba all the way up to York Factory.

Norway House detachment was an isolated community, accessible up to 1977 only by waterway from the south, and by a local Manitoba airline. Needless to say, when the teachers and nurses flew back into Norway House to start a new season of work in September, they were given a welcome by the local constables, who usually met the incoming aircraft to conduct an inspection for illegal spirits being brought to the Native Reserve (which was a "dry" community).

Policing other inland communities was done mainly by the ten single Norway House constables, who would fly out on a rotational basis in a single engine aircraft. They were dropped off at their communities for a seven-day period. The communities usually had two Band constables to assist the officer in his investigations, and they were also his backup should something serious arise, which was not uncommon. Bear in mind these constables were not armed; their ability to deal with problems rested on common sense and quick thinking. In these isolated communities the local RCMP officer was called upon to be a social worker, police officer, mailman, and jail guard. Many investigations, including serious shootings and assaults, were brought on by the consumption of "bean juice," a form of liquor made mostly of a fruit mash. People paid up to $120 for a twelve-ounce bottle of bootlegged liquor. Aside from the legal matters, the police officer, when time permitted, was able to join in community celebrations and give talks to the local school children. In the springtime he managed to drop everything and head to the river systems and spend a day fishing for rainbow trout and lake trout, which were in abundance.

After seven days in the isolated communities, an officer was blessed with four days off before going back to work. It was on one of these four days off that I recall four young men paddling across the Nelson River toward the RCMP "Point" on a day that was not even fit for a dog to be outside. As they approached the wharf another constable and I looked at each other and muttered, "Who are those fools, trying to make it to shore with high waves and nasty weather going against them?" Upon hitting the wharf with their canoes, four wet and soggy souls crawled out onto the land.

Later, we invited them up to the police station, which also had a single men's quarters attached to it on the back. Being single and ready for a party, we called around to the teachers and nurses, and what the heck, the traveling circuit court was also at Norway House. They could not leave because of the weather, so we invited them to spend some time with our weary travelers. A great time was had by all.

While in Norway House, our guests had the opportunity to meet other members of the community and were welcomed as if they had been there for years. One remembers taking the guys over to an old conservation officer's home on an island to meet the infamous "Denny Allen." Now, when first meeting this individual, one would have believed they had met a troll from under the bridge, as he wouldn't give a person the time of day. However, as you got used to him, and when he learned of what these four travelers were doing, he opened up his book of secrets on traveling the waterways. I recall Denny asking me on several occasions whether those "young bucks" had made it to their final destination.

I spent three years in Norway House as a police officer, and later moved north to the Northwest Territories with my bride—who I met in Norway House. Yes, she was a teacher. We enjoyed our time in that community and have never forgotten it or its people. When I got a telephone call from Dennis, it took a bit of time to think back twenty-eight years, but when he sent me a photograph of the bunch, things sure came back in a hurry!

—Mal

Lonna Chale
(*Lonna and Shelly, Pembina, North Dakota*)

I WAS BORN in Mayville, North Dakota, in 1963, to Karen and Iran Johnson. At the age of six, my parents moved my sister Debbie, brother Darin, and me to Cavalier, North Dakota. My dad worked for the U.S. Customs Service and was on the road a lot, and Cavalier had doctors and a hospital, so he decided that would be a good place to live. We later moved to Pembina, where I lived until graduating from high school in 1981. My parents still live in Pembina, and I have returned with my own family.

Pembina is a town where two rivers meet, and we did "typical kids things" such as swinging from a rope into the Pembina River. We jumped off the bridge and sunk in the mud at the bottom of the river. I guess as kids we didn't realize what dangers this might have produced.

In 1979, I was sixteen. One of my best friends was Shelly Korbel, and we worked at the Tastee Freeze (my mom's first job outside of the home in Pembina was at the Tastee Freeze). Pembina is a quiet little town of 600 people, with no theater or other avenues of entertainment, so Shelly and I, as well as our other friends, created our own. One day while working at the Tastee Freeze, in walked these wayward boaters, who we began teasing and harassing. They had been paddling down the river to Hudson Bay. One of the guys must have thought Shelly and I were cute, and began flirting with us, so we added two or three years to our ages to impress him. We thought he was cute and a lot of fun! His name was Dennis and he seemed harmless, so we invited him to my parents' home.

Mom treated him to lemonade and cookies. I am sure as an impressionable sixteen-year-old, I listened intently to Dennis' story about the river trip—possibly flirting while watching my mother out of the corner of my eye to see her reaction. Remember, I was sixteen, and an older boy seemed interested in me. Wow! I guess Mom approved of how the evening was going because I don't remember any major lectures. She appeared to understand the situation, probably because mothers seem to be that way, whereas a father's first reaction is to screen the boy very carefully as to his intentions.

I think I take after my mother in that we are both pretty adventurous. This has given me many experiences, such as a chance meeting with a river traveler years ago. Now that I have kids, I wonder whether they will be like me. I really want my kids to experience life, but as a parent I now face the things I never worried about before—fear of something happening to my kids. Sometimes my dad says "what goes around, comes around." I want my kids to be inquisitive, but careful—still having an outgoing personality, but tempered with common sense—something very hard for a sixteen-year-old to grasp. As my kids go through life, I hope each meets a special traveler on a wayward journey, and I hope that I can be a mother who stands watch over them, but at a distance.

Les Palm
(Nielsville, Minnesota)

I WAS BORN in 1955, one of six sons of DeForest and Anna Mae Palm. Of Swedish and Norwegian descent, I have lived in Nielsville, Minnesota, all my life. I grew up on a farm, and have done a lot of different jobs, from farming to construction to driving a harvester.

I met these four guys when they stopped to rest at my grandparents farm along the Red River, about fifty miles north of Fargo, North Dakota. They were going into a town that was close to the river to have something to eat, so I gave them a ride. It was about 6 or 7 P.M., and I was done with work for the day, so I was heading in to have a beer. We had a beer together—okay, one beer led to two or three more.

One of the guys was tall and we were talking about basketball, because he was a coach, I think. So as the night went on we talked, and then I said I had a place to play some ball. It was in a barn we had at my place, and we went to play at about 1 A.M.

I don't know why we did it, but it was a fun time. Maybe they needed something different to do from just rowing down the river.

I guess I must have made an impression on them to look me up after all these years. I was glad to make some new friends.

I don't think they felt too good the next day. I know I didn't.

Bob Friederichs
(Foxhome, Minnesota)

OUR FARM WAS purchased by my grandparents in 1889. In the first half of the 1900s there were many more curves and oxbows in the river. Trees lined all of the riverbanks. In 1953 the river was straightened and dredged for about twenty miles, starting east of our farm and up to Breckenridge. Our parents built most of the buildings on the farm. My brother John and I took over the farming operation in 1962. In 1989 our son, Pete, and John's son, Mike, started operating the farm. Our grandchildren are the fifth generation to live here.

We first noticed your group when we were sitting at the supper table and one of the girls noticed there was something coming down the river. A short time later there was a knock on the door, which surprised us a little as we had not seen any vehicles go by. You asked if you could camp on the farmstead by the river, which we were glad to accommodate. I believe a couple of our boys came over to your campsite to help gather firewood. The comments the next day were on how clean you left the campsite—it was almost as if no one had camped there.

We were all interested and excited about your planned trip, and really appreciated the card you sent after reaching your destination. Many times there were memories of your stopping by on your long trip to Hudson Bay. You boys are always welcome to stop in anytime.